Bears, Packrats, & Bikers

lessons learned from fear

by
WILLIAM H. COX

Unless otherwise indicated, all scripture was taken from the King James Version of the Bible.

ISBN: 978-1-7342790-0-9

Copyright 2018 by William H. Cox
All rights reserved under International Copyright Law.
Cover Photos/Design copyright by William H. Cox

Edited by GraphiComm Inc., Cocolalla, ID

Other books written by William H. Cox

Skies Are Not Cloudy All Day
– *Is God trying to get your attention?*

The unconditional love of
A Dog's Love

The Last Cast
– *Proactively fishing with grace*

These books available on Amazon & the website below:
www.rustyironranchllc.com

Contact:
Rusty Iron Ranch, LLC.
P.O. Box 1582
Sandpoint, Idaho 83864
e-mail: *jumpcreek113@yahoo.com*

All rights reserved. No part of this publication may be reproduced without express written consent of the publisher.

BEARS, PACKRATS, & BIKERS

lessons learned from fear

Bear	7
Shadow of Death	13
One of Those Days	23
Authority	41
Winter Camping	49
The Mountain Car	65
Inner Walls	75
Hitching a Ride	89
Acknowledgements	109

This book is dedicated to my friend Chris Nicolls

The trial he is going through is a big one.

I admire his faith and confidence,

knowing that he is a child of God.

"The fear of the LORD *is* the beginning of wisdom,
And the knowledge of the Holy One *is* understanding."

Proverbs 9:10

Bear!

2 Timothy 1:7

" For God has not given us a spirit of fear, but of power and of love and of a sound mind."

The well-worn path seemed harmless enough. Filtered sunlight showed orange through the gently flickering leaves. The scent of pine intermingled with campfire smoke filled the air. Voices of other children playing echoed through the trees surrounding the campsite.

Being the oldest of the siblings, it was me and Monica's chore to get water from the stream to do the dishes after supper. As we neared the stream, each of us carrying a bucket, the running water covered our whispers of retaliation.

"You know he is going to try to scare us, don't you?" Monica whispered.

"Not this time!" I replied firmly.

Arriving at the edge of the stream, I searched for a good spot to get clean water. Typically, the deeper the water, the fewer floaties ended up in the bucket.

I found a deep spot next to an eddy in the small stream where I could dip the bucket completely, ensuring clean water. Kneeling on one knee in the soft green moss, I braced my left hand on a partially submerged rock. As I plunged the red plastic bucket into the deep hole, I watched how the water swirled inside.

From her post as lookout, Monica scanned the bushes behind us for any sign of impending danger. My legs were tense in anticipation, ready for any signal to jump to safety, even if that meant to the other side of the creek. My plan for escape constantly adapted to the changing circumstances.

All our senses were keenly aware of our surroundings. A water ouzel popped out from under the water with a large stonefly in its mouth. It bobbed up and down several times before flying off to feed the ample morsel to its young. A small brook trout hit the surface in the pool above us with nothing more than a swirl of the water. Off in the distance, a pileated woodpecker cackled through large ponderosa pines up the hill. The scent of woodsmoke from camp provided a hint of security. Nothing got past our observations.

Water spilled over the rim of the bucket as I pulled it up from the pool. Monica grabbed the handle from me, exchanging it with the other empty bucket.

Lifting the second bucket from the stream, I stood up and sighed deeply, glancing over at Monica. I felt the nausea laying in the pit of her stomach, too, as I bravely led the way back to camp. With each step, I scoured the heavy brush alongside the trail, searching for any sign that might expose his devious plan. Anticipation built with each step, tightening the springs of anxiety into a twisted coil of potential panic. The possibility of unseen danger lurked behind every heavy leaf-bearing limb.

The closer we got to camp, the thicker it hung in the air. My white knuckles were numb with the death grip I had on the handle.

Suddenly from behind us, the brush parted with a roar. "GRRAUGHHHHH!" Dad erupted out with hands high in the air.

Monica let out a blood-curdling scream which only added to the intensity of the moment. Dropping her bucket, she dowsed both of us before heading to camp in a blur.

Adrenaline-laced horror shot through my veins. My heart met my ears, thundering loudly, blurring my vision with fright. As pre-planned, I swung my bucket. like a discus athlete. Using the momentum of the swing, I launched the bucket straight at Dad with everything I had. It sailed over his head, collided into a large lodgepole pine and collapsed in a brilliant shower of water, backlit by the last few rays of sunlight.

Within seconds, I had passed Monica down the beaten path to the safety of the campfire. Dad dodged the bucket, laughing. After retrieving them, he refilled the one good bucket at the creek so Mom could do dishes.

Later that night, as we were crawling into our U.S. Army- issued, down-filled, mummy-type sleeping bags, I pleaded with Monica. "Please don't scream tonight. I hate it when you do that."

"Well, I can't help it when I think a bear is going to get me," she responded defiantly.

Honestly, I didn't like that thought either, but preferred not to let my thoughts go there.

Gazing out the front of the small backpacking tent to the bright orange glow, I said as reassuringly as possible, "No bears are going to come close to this fire."

We both watched the golden glow flicker off the surrounding trees. Eventually, unable to keep our eyes open, we drifted off into a deep sleep.

Monica was a restless sleeper. She tossed and turned over and over several times throughout the night.

Right around the darkest part of the night, she whispered. "Bill, are you awake?"

"Yes...What?" I prepared myself for whatever she was about to say.

"A bear has my legs." There was a touch of trembling in her voice.

Instant fear shot through my body, knowing what was about to be unleashed. "NO, MONICA! A bear DOES NOT have you," I replied firmly. If she heard even the slightest quiver in my voice, it was all over.

Trying to work free from her mummy bag bound her even tighter, which tripped the trigger on the most blood-curdling scream known to man. "A BEAR'S GOT ME!"

Her scream shattered the stillness of the night, echoing down the quiet little stream and throughout the entire forest. I am sure Monica's screaming is why we always had to camp so far off the beaten path. It was just too embarrassing for my parents the next day.

Instinctively, self-preservation kicked in. I hit the bottom of my sleeping bag and playing dead, frozen in the fetal position, hands covering the back of my neck. I figured to play it safe. If a bear did have her, it would be full by the time it got around to me!

We all encounter fear in our lives. It starts at a young age and plagues us throughout our lives. Most often, it is self-induced with our gifted imaginations or on occasion is a very real terrifying experience. Either way that terror can follow us the rest of our lives continually haunting us.

The Bible says in Isaiah 41:10, "So do not fear, for I am with you; do not be dismayed, for I am your God. I will strengthen you; I will uphold you in my righteous hand."

In context, God is saying that He has called you to be His servant. For you *to be called*, there would have to be a God. God in this verse is possessively active; i.e., *I am with you; I am your God*. That would mean you would have to *believe* that He is your God, right? To believe takes faith. Faith in God who cannot be seen. So that scripture says that if you have faith in God—who is unseen—you will be dismayed, and He will strengthen you.

Consequently, there is nothing you must do in this equation except to believe and have faith. The rest is up for God to do. That sounds easy enough, but it wasn't always that easy for me.

Shadow of Death

Psalm 34:4

"I prayed to the Lord, and He answered me. He freed me from all my fears."

When I pulled into the empty trailhead parking lot, I was surprised at the lack of snow. There were patches of open sagebrush hillside which were completely bare. This sure was going to throw a kink in my plans for cross-country skiing the outskirts of Yellowstone Park. I had seen grizzly bear tracks up the remote valley the previous fall while elk-hunting. I figured bears would be hibernating and wanted to use spring break at Montana State University to scout the country for potential elk-hunting in the fall.

I had experienced panic attacks during the last semester of school and wondered if maybe working full-time along with taking a full load of credits was stressing me out too much. I figured a winter camping trip by myself in the backcountry might get my nerves back in order.

The trail was mostly clear, so I strapped my skis to the back of the backpack and headed up the trail. I was excited to see a moose was using the trail as well. I hoped to catch a glimpse of it in the next few days.

I was familiar with the trail since I had hunted this remote valley several times the previous fall. It caught my attention when the moose tracks cut off the manmade trail and went down through the bottom of draw avoiding an exposed outcropping of rock. Why hadn't the moose stuck to the trail? I realized why when I found myself standing on a slab of solid ice that sloped down to a twenty-five-foot cliff. Water from a spring crossed the trail during the day, then froze overnight. When I realized the predicament I was in, I stopped immediately, hoping my boots would hold. As I contemplated my escape route, I noticed the moose tracks far below me in the snow at the base of the cliff. I laughed momentarily about how much wiser the moose was than me. *I am losing my edge*, I thought.

When I turned to go back down the trail, the skis on my backpack hit the steep hillside pushing me towards the cliff's edge. I quickly used my poles to catch the mishap. Every toe went on alert, desperately grabbing for a foothold. I slowly turned around the opposite direction with my back and skis away from the slope and gingerly walked back to solid ground.

I scolded myself hard. That was too close and a stupid mistake to make when I was by myself. I needed to pay attention and get my backwoods mind working again. I had gotten soft over the winter.

I worked my way up the trail a couple of miles to an open hillside which overlooked the wide-open valley below me. The valley floor was covered in snow, dissected in half by a band of red willows. Majestic snow-covered peaks in Yellowstone Park rose up beyond the remote high valley. This would be my spring retreat for the next few days.

The southwestern hillside was void of snow, which made wood readily available for a campfire. I had planned on using my one-burner cook stove for cooking dinner, but due to the lack of snow, that night I was having steak on a willow stick cooked over the coals of a campfire.

Three stunted lodgepole pine trees within twenty-five yards of my camp served as sentinels overlooking the valley below. I briefly thought of storing my extra food in a bag and hoisting it up into one of the trees in the event a grizzly stopped by unannounced. I opted out of that decision since it was the middle of March, and I was certain the bears were deep in their midwinter slumber.

As the sun dipped low in the clear Montana sky, the temperature followed suit. The popping fire was a welcome sound breaking the otherwise silent landscape. I had gathered enough wood for several days. The warm orange glow from the fire perfectly complemented the cold blue hues of the snow-covered mountains. It all came together with elk steak and pre-baked potato. As if on cue, a lone coyote began barking on a distant ridge as I opened the chocolate pudding for dessert. Another answered on the opposite side of the valley. Witnessing the transition of the evening shadows at sunset into the finale of the Milky Way stirred my soul. There had to be a God that set everything in place so perfectly.

That thought stirred me deeply. I felt obligated to at least look at this whole God thing on this trip. Before leaving, I had thrown a Bible in my backpack at the last minute. My little sister had sent it to me and had encouraged me to read it.

I had tried to read the Bible many times, although honestly, it was usually after a night of staying out late at the bar, when I could only read with one eye due to the polluted state I was in. The recent panic attacks had persuaded me to take a more sober look at the subject of faith. I hoped that reading the Bible on this trip might reveal something about the God my sisters spoke so highly of. There had to be something to it, because it was obvious to me they had something I didn't have. There was something real there, but why was it such a mystery? Why was God so elusive? Or was He? Maybe I was such a rotten sinner He wouldn't let me in. I joked about it often, that if I ever went into a church it would probably cave in on me.

What I had read of the Bible sure made me feel convicted. I couldn't get very far without seeing how much of a sinner I was. I also couldn't see how anyone could do good all the time. It just seemed impossible. Still, I argued, I was a decent guy. I knew that. I tried to be, anyway. I could convince myself of my basic decency most of the time, until I read the Bible. What was it that my sisters saw that I couldn't see?

I took my pants and shirt off before crawling into my cold sleeping bag. I lay in it, waiting for the cold material to warm up before I moved again. I had learned early on to keep my water bottle in my sleeping bag with me so it wouldn't freeze. The food, frying pan, and stove were next to me in the tent. I watched a giant full moon emerge over the mountain, lighting up the valley below as the embers in the fire died out. Sweet sleep came swiftly.

At precisely 1:05 A.M., I awoke abruptly, straining to hear. I saw nothing but straining to hear caused my heartbeat to race. Something wasn't right, but I couldn't put my finger on it. Hearing nothing, I closed my eyes. My heartbeat had nearly returned to normal when the sound came to me.

"Uuunghhh..." sounded through the cold clear air. Looking out the front of the tent to the large moonlit valley below me, I strained to see the source of the strange sound. I tried hard to convince myself that it was the moose whose tracks I had seen the day before. I listened closely to confirm that observation, but my heartbeat was so loud I couldn't make a firm decision. The source of the noise was a long way off, although it seemed to be getting closer. I reasonably surveyed this situation. I didn't have a gun or pepper spray, and all my food was in my tent. Steak drippings most likely were on the pants that I was using for a pillow. The nearest tree was twenty-five yards away in the direction of the approaching animal.

"Uuunghhh..." it sounded again, much closer. My heart started racing. My mouth was dry, and I swallowed hard.

"Don't panic!" I reminded myself.

Then I heard it walking laboriously in the crusty snow. The raspy heavy breathing unnerved me. In and out. I listened hard trying to decode this guessing game. The animal appeared to be circling the tent. There had to be a simple explanation for this strange sound that didn't have the word *grizzly* in it. When it stopped downwind of the tent, I struggled hard not to panic. It was time for action of some kind on my part or I would be involved in my own fatality, and it needed to be done fast. I knew what it was and needed to stop playing mind games with myself. This situation had become critical!

I grabbed the frying pan and swung down hard on my camp stove several times, then listened intently. All I heard was ringing in my ears. Had it left, I wondered? I slowly unzipped the door to the tent, peering outside for any clues. It was so quiet it hurt.

Suddenly a deep guttural "Gruunghhh..." sounded from behind the tent. I had to make a move now. The creature had not just circled the tent; it had moved closer towards me. I had one shot at getting into the tree twenty-five yards away. The problem was, all I had on was my long handles, and I was barefoot. It could be a long night, sitting in a tree in single digits.

Remembering the Bible my sister had given me, I gripped it firmly, hoping that would bring me good luck. With my other hand I reached for the only reasonable source of protection I had: the frying pan. If it came down to it, I would get in one good swing! I crawled out of the tent and looked towards the ridge. There was a large dark shape against the skyline. In the deepest voice I could muster I yelled, "Get outta here. I'm trying to sleep!"

I heard a strange clacking sound, like teeth, and then with a woof the big bear took off bucking down the ridge to the valley below. My legs shook uncontrollably, mostly from fear and a little from the below-freezing temperatures. I crawled back into my sleeping bag. For the next hour, I strained to hear any sound outside. Eventually, the effort of listening wore me out, and I fell asleep.

I awoke late the next morning to snowmobilers driving through the big meadow below. I got dressed and went out to the ridge where everything had happened during the night. The bear tracks were over ten inches long and had completely circled my tent. So much for a relaxing retreat in the backcountry, I thought. I was now more anxious than ever.

When I got back to the tent, I picked up the Bible. Again, it made no sense. I just could not figure out why my sisters thought so highly of this book. All it made me see is that I was a hopeless sinner and headed straight for hell. There was no hope whatsoever. In disgust, I threw the book aside.

I spent another night despite the grizzly encounter, but this time I left all my food outside. I didn't have enough rope to suspend it in the tree, so I left it at the base instead. That night was miserable. Between a couple of coyotes fighting over my squeeze bottle of Parkay margarine and an over-amorous owl, I couldn't get any sleep.

Even though it made no sense to me at the time, the message I read in the Bible that day in my tent was spot-on with how I was living my life. I was a sinner headed straight for hell, but the circumstances in which God allowed the grizzly to show up that night did partially what they were supposed to: draw me to God. The same was true with the panic attacks. Both the grizzly and the panic attacks provoked fear that eventually drew me to God, albeit in a roundabout way because I was stubborn and wanted to do it my way, not God's way. Instead of putting my faith in Jesus, I put it in the Bible, like a good luck charm. I wanted an easy fix with no commitment, something I could use when I needed help without changing my lifestyle. In reality, I was, running away from Him with my fingers in my ears.

After that camping trip, I increased my drinking of alcohol to deal with the panic attacks, which in turn made them more intense. The alcohol and the panic attacks fed off each other for fifteen years.

When I finally got around to acknowledging Jesus, it was through faith. Not by faith in the Bible to protect me, but faith in Jesus to protect me. The Bible won't save you, but the author will. Jesus, through the Holy Spirit, inspired men over two thousand years to write it. Therefore, they call the Bible the Living Word.

It is a crazy thing, but when you accept through faith that Jesus died for you, acknowledging that He paid the price for your sins and call upon His name, He indwells your soul.

Romans10:13 "Whosoever calls on the name of the Lord shall be saved."

You are then a child of God. He lives inside of you. He enables you to read the Bible, understand what it says, and follow its instruction you as you walk through life.

One of Those Days

Matthew 6:34

"Therefore do not worry about tomorrow, for tomorrow will worry about itself. Each day has enough trouble of its own."

The lodgepole pine snag swayed back and forth wildly under the Bell helicopter's rotors' thunderous *whop, whop, whop* wind thrust. We still had 100 feet before we would be on the ground. If the snag snapped or one of the branches broke free and hit one of the blades, we would be on the ground in a matter of seconds. Tyler looked over at me nervously. He had a similar snag waving outside his window as well. He made the sign of the cross. I nodded with both hands in a praying position. We both had helmets with mics which let us communicate with the pilot, but he didn't need to hear our play-by-play action going on from the back seat. The Bell helicopter was reeking with tension.

The warning "This is a tight one, boys!" came through the earphones. "When we get on the ground, these two snags and the three in front of us have to go down before I can get out of this hover hole."

I pushed the button to speak. "Affirmative."

I watched out the window as the grass in the small meadow swirled erratically below us, whipping back and forth. As we met the last ten feet of our descent, dust and debris blew up from the Bell's rotors encasing us in a self-induced dust storm. In seconds, we were safe on the ground. Tyler and I opened the doors. Ducking low beneath the blades, we retrieved our gear and hauled it back out of the way. Tyler and I had already decided who would clear the landing site. I chose scissors and Tyler came up with paper. I had won or lost, depending on how you looked at it. Clearing a landing pad of "widow-maker snags" with a Bell helicopter sitting in proximity made you earn your pay. We had two more firefighters over the hill in McCall, waiting for transport. Clearing the helispot would ensure everyone's safety.

Landing the helicopter into the tight pocket amongst these trees was relatively easy, but to successfully take off out of it, the pilot needed the rotors thrust forward to lift- off. It didn't help that we were also in the bottom of a narrow drainage with steep mountains on three sides.

I worked as swiftly as possible, dropping the tall trees around the little meadow. After Tyler and I had cleared most of the loose brush, we signaled the pilot. As he fired up the helicopter, we put on our goggles and covered our faces with handkerchiefs to protect us from the airborne debris. Within minutes, the helicopter flew up and over the ridge, and we were left standing in the remote meadow in complete silence.

Removing our handkerchiefs, Tyler was the first to speak. "That was crazy!"

"Yeah, I thought that snag was coming down!"

"He's a good pilot. I guess he flew in Vietnam," Tyler said, lighting up a smoke. "It's over that ridge, huh?" Tyler motioned up a steep, brush-infested hillside.

"Yup! I guess we better get there before that thing blows up." I removed the saw chaps for the difficult climb.

While I double-checked my pack, Tyler wrapped the chaps around the bar on the chainsaw. He threw the saw over his shoulder, grabbed his Pulaski in the other hand, and headed up the steep hill. I grabbed the saw gas and oil along with my Pulaski and followed.

On the way in, the pilot had circled both snags that had taken a lightning strike. The one we were most concerned about was on a southwest facing slope. It was a giant ponderosa pine which was starting to smoke pretty good midway up the tree. We needed to drop the tree to the ground before afternoon winds spread sparks across the dry southwest-facing slope.

Typical for July and August, we hadn't seen rain for weeks. The dry-lightning storm which had come through ten days earlier left a large swath of fires popping up across central Idaho, through the Frank Church Wilderness into Montana. We had been fighting fire for over a week. They would fly us in; we would put them out, and then move on to the next one.

The only thing good about the steep hill we were climbing was that it was on the north slope. It was a little cooler than out in the sun, but the brush we had to fight to the top was brutal.

Tyler reached the top before I did. He amazed me. He was the only guy I knew that could climb a hill that steep, smoking a cigarette and light another at the top. Tyler was a sawyer from way back. He was a good asset to the D-6 Fisheries Hotshots, which was what we called ourselves.

When I reached the top of the ridge, the helicopter passed over the lightning strike, carrying the two remaining members of our crew, Sam and John. They would hike up quickly since they didn't have to pack anything but their packs and pulaskis. The smoking ponderosa stood halfway down the hill from where Tyler and I were standing. We waited until Sam and John had unloaded before relaying to them the best route to our location.

Sam arrived first. He said John was filling two bladder bags at the creek and would be up shortly.

Upon surveying the situation, we could knock this fire out in short order as long as everything went as planned. Elk had been using a spring nearby to cool off in the hot August sun. Bulls often used these sites during the pre-rut wallowing, which created small ponds. Since there was no other water nearby to help extinguish the fire, this spring would be our water source. The proximity was such that if we dropped the tree perfectly, it would land directly in the wallow. If not, it could get ugly fast.

Tyler and I flipped a coin to determine who would drop the tree. Tyler won the coin toss. He was putting on the chaps as John found us. One look at John got all our attention. He didn't look well. His face was beet-red, and he was starting to get dizzy. We recognized the signs of heat exhaustion. Tyler and I grabbed the bladder bags he was packing, and Sam promptly escorted him to shade out of the way. Sam instructed him to sit tight to cool off in the shade. He had him elevate his feet and sip on water. Sam stayed with John, while I spotted Tyler sawing.

Before he started, Tyler sharpened his Stihl 038 and made sure that his escape route was clear. Then he cut a wedge from a limb nearby and laid it next to the base of the tree. When he was ready, he looked at me, smiled a big toothy grin, and nodded his head. I'd grabbed a small stick that I could throw at Tyler in the event a problem arose he couldn't see. I raised my hand with the stick showing that I had him covered.

It was exciting to see Tyler in action. Born and raised in central Idaho, he had been a sawyer most of his younger years. The Stihl 038 seemed like an extension of his hand.

Long ribbons of sawdust flew from the saw as he made the face cut. He knocked the "V" portion loose, then repositioned himself to the back of the tree to start the final back cut. The butt of the tree was almost 48 inches across on the big tree, so Tyler had to work from both sides with the 36" bar to make the final cut. The steep slope made it difficult to maneuver side to side. When he had cut halfway through, he took the wedge and with the back of his ax knocked it into the cut. The wedge ensured the tree would not set back on the bar which would bind up the saw.

I fixed my eyes on the smoldering lightning strike. Occasionally a shower of sparks would fall landing across Tyler's shoulders. I kept my eye out for any unusual movement in case the top of the tree or any large falling debris busted loose from above. As the saw got closer to the face cut, Tyler glanced in my direction and up the tree. Any second the tree should pop. The anticipation was rising for all of us. With the saw still in the cut Tyler took his ax out and hit the wedge.

Suddenly the large tree popped and shuddered. Tyler tried to pull the saw from the cut, but the tree had sat down on the bar. Tyler had one hand on the saw to pull it free once the tree started going over. Out of nowhere, a stiff breeze came upslope. Tyler looked at me in disgust and shook his head. The massive tree slowly started to spin on the stump, then gradually began to fall up the hill opposite the elk wallow. I hollered at Tyler to get out of there. Tyler left the saw stuck in the tree and scrambled away from the base of the tree in a cloud of dust. Once I saw Tyler was heading out, I sidehilled in the opposite direction.

The mighty ponderosa gained momentum as it neared the ground. The wind rushing through the pine needles made a loud *whoosh*. The middle of the tree hit a rock outcropping with a loud *whomp*, sending dust and debris shooting into the air. The tree responded like a teeter-totter, catapulting the butt of the tree 50 feet in the air with a powerful surge. I saw Tyler's yellow fire shirt out of the corner of my eye, scrambling sidehill. The butt slammed down hard where Tyler had been running seconds before. The percussion as it hit the ground shook the mountain, knocking Tyler to the ground before sending the butt bouncing again high in the air. Gravity kicked in, causing the tree to slide swiftly down the steep hill. The rock outcrop caught the tree at the midpoint, causing it to shift sidehill while rolling downhill in my direction.

When the top of the tree hit the steep slope, it exploded, sending sparks across the hillside, immediately erupting in dust, smoke and bursting into flames.

The rolling tree rolled quickly in my direction. I didn't have time to change directions or try to outrun it. The middle of the tree would overtake me in a matter of seconds. I dove for a small outcropping of rock, hoping the tree would bounce over me. I tucked myself close against the hillside, trying to make myself flat. A shower of rock and dust showered over me, and then nothing. I slowly lifted my head to see that a large limb had stuck in the ground, sticking the huge tree to the mountain. Seizing the opportunity, I leapt from the security of my fortress and headed back to the others.

Tyler looked at me with a smile and wide eyes. "You okay?"

I nodded "Yeah, man, I thought you were toast there for a second!"

Tyler laughed his hearty laugh. "Yeah, me too!"

Sam and John joined us, and we formed a plan to scratch a line around the sides of the fire before it went over the top of the ridge. By now it was close to 5:00 P.M. As the evening progressed, we hoped the downslope winds would begin to work to our advantage.

John's face had regained its color, but to play it safe, we put him on the back of the line. Since Tyler already had the chaps on, he took the front position, sawing a swath through the brush. Sam helped clear the brush, then John and I used pulaskis to scratch in a fire line. The higher we worked up the hill, the hotter the flames became. Thick smoke made our noses run and our eyes water uncontrollably, leaving watermarks down our soot-covered faces. Sweat continually dripped off our noses and into our eyes.

As we had hoped, the downslope winds aided our efforts when the sun dropped behind the mountain, instantly stopping the fire's advance. Before long, we had isolated the section of the tree that was on fire and cleared away most of the fuels. By midnight, the fire had died down, and we decided to take a break.

At the top of the one-acre fire was a bench created by a root wad from a tree that had blown over many years ago. Over the years, it had filled in with soil and debris, forming a level spot where we could all sit on the steep hillside.

We all dug into our packs to refuel our bodies with a variety of quick, ready-to-eat snacks. I ate a combination of nuts and berries with a can of smoked oysters that had been on my mind for the last few hours. We were all exhausted and spoke little, sitting in the pitch-black night. We'd switched our headlamps off, so the only light came from the few coals flickering in the center of the fire. Occasionally a flame would pop up, providing a little more light. The smoke had all but disappeared. Stars lit up the sky, but there was no moon. The mountains that lay before us were completely black.

Suddenly we heard something breaking brush below. I turned on my headlamp to see two glowing eyes at the bottom of the fire.

'Oh, looky there, Smokey showed up!" I said.

"For dinner, probably," Sam answered.

Tyler said, "Yeah, he wants some of your oysters!"

I shut my headlamp off, and the small bear rummaged around below us while we ate. Then he disappeared.

No one had the energy to hike back to the helispot to get our sleeping bags, so we decided to get a little sleep on the level spot where we ate supper. There was exactly enough room for the four of us to lie down with our heads facing the fire and feet to the mountain. It didn't take long before we were all fast asleep. Tyler was the first; his snoring shook the mountain.

Sometime in the night, I got a whiff of something terrible. I remember thinking about how putrid Tyler's breath was. Then I felt something wet on my ear and forehead. I had a vague recollection that it might be the bear licking the salt from the sweat on my face. I was so tired, I pushed its head away and turned over, covering my face with my arm. I figured if the bear woke Tyler, it would be in for a world of hurt.

The cold predawn air worked through our fire shirts, waking us a few hours later. Only a few wisps of smoke surfaced throughout the one-acre fire. Now we searched earnestly for a hot spot to build a fire to ward off the chill until the sun came up over the ridge. John found one and was able to get a small fire going. We all huddled around its warmth, using the now-welcome flames to boil water for coffee and oatmeal.

Sam's pack was missing. That's when I remembered the little bear in the middle of the night. We looked around, and the proof was everywhere around where we'd slept. Sam's pack had been dragged into some brush a little way down the hill. One of the pack's straps was hung up on a Ponderosa pine limb. Upon further investigation, we saw that the brave little bear had rummaged through John's pack too and had run off with a few his candy bars and some jerky.

We discussed the plans for the day over breakfast. John and I would stay on this fire to knock out the few remaining hot spots while Tyler and Sam went down the ridge to take care of the other lightning strike. John and I would join them when we were finished mopping up.

They located the other lightning strike about five hundred yards down the hill in a small basin. There was a wet spring below it, as at the first lightning strike. Tyler wanted a chance to redeem himself after the last tree-falling disaster. The Douglas fir was easily one-quarter of the size of the Ponderosa, and the cool morning air worked in Tyler's favor. He had no problem dropping the snag perfectly into the spring. Within a couple of hours, he and Sam had the smoldering tree mopped up and cold to the touch.

Sam called in on the radio to tell dispatch we had put both fires out. Tom, our supervisor, got on the radio and asked us to stay on the fire throughout the day to make sure no other smokes popped up. He had heard about the hover hole and requested all of us to lighten our loads as much as possible before the helicopter picked us up the next morning.

We stayed on the fires until six o'clock that night. After the sun dropped behind the ridge, we followed it over the hill to the helispot. That night we gorged on everything in our pack and drank all our water.

The next morning, a different pilot from New Meadows flew over to pick the first two of us up and radioed back to the dispatcher in McCall reporting that the helispot was too dangerous to fly out of. Tom, called me on the radio, since I had cleared the helispot and reported the bad news. I answered back, explaining how Tyler and I had cleared several trees out to make it much safer than when we'd landed. Tom asked me to stand by but informed us that we should be prepared to hike out to the Southfork of the Salmon River Road. The crew's faces showed how unpopular that option was. We had eaten every morsel of food and unloaded all our water and were over ten air miles away from the Southfork Road in some of the roughest country in Central Idaho. It would take us a good day of hard hiking in 95 degree temperatures to get out from where we were.

While we were waiting to hear back from Tom, John found a huckleberry patch nearby. The purple huckleberries were juicy and huge. Some were as big as our thumbs. We all started filling our water bottles, figuring that we would probably be sustaining ourselves off huckleberries for the next couple of days.

Suddenly we heard a helicopter approaching around the ridge. Sam and I went to the helispot to direct the pilot. We already had strips of flagging in the trees to show the pilot wind direction and intensity. The pilot dropped into the helispot with ease. It was the Vietnam Veteran pilot who had initially dropped us into the spot.

He requested we take out all the gear in the first load; then he would come back to fly out the two lightest guys. By the time he returned for Tyler and me, he had used up most of his fuel weight to compensate for the extra weight to lift us out of the hover hole.

As Tyler and I buckled our seat belt harnesses, he turned and said, "Ready?"

We both nodded, and he said with a smile, "I sure hope we have enough fuel; we're cutting it close."

I was never so glad to be back on the ground at Krassel. The way this fire had gone, nothing would have surprised me. When we reached the Krassel landing strip, the pilot said he could fly the lightest one of us over the hill to McCall. The flight would take about half an hour. The rest of the crew would have to drive over, and that would take two hours on rough roads in a crew cab. We had all been arguing over who was the lightest. We all had lost quite a bit of weight since the lightning storm had started the fires. Each of us stepped on the scale to check our weight, and I happened to be the lightest, beating Tyler by half a pound. At the beginning of the fire, Tyler and I had weighed the most, and by the end, we were the lightest.

After we landed in McCall, I swung by Paul's Market to buy myself the biggest steak I could find. My wife, Julie, had been fighting fire with her crew on the Buckhorn fire in the same Southfork of the Salmon River complex. Her crew was still hard at it, so I would be dining alone at our Forest Service housing in New Meadows. We were renting a house next door to the ranger and his wife. He was busy overseeing fire duties on his district while his wife had gone back east to visit family. No one had been around to take care of the lawn for over ten days. It was overgrown and very dry.

My focus was on that big steak. I felt like a new man after a long hot shower and a clean shave. Shedding the Nomex fire gear in exchange for clean Levi's and t-shirt was like losing ten pounds of black ground-in soot.

There was a small concrete pad on the back of the porch. We had recently obtained a barbeque from a family member but had yet to use it. I turned on the propane and used the automatic starter to fire it up. *We're living uptown now*, I thought.

After letting the grill warm up for a bit, I dropped the large T-bone on the hot clean grill. The sizzling steak tantalized my taste buds. I watched the barbeque for a little while to see how well it worked and went inside to check on the baked potato in the microwave. When I returned, smoke was billowing out of the barbeque. As I lifted the lid, the steak burst into flames. I stuck it with the long barbeque fork and flipped it over, revealing a dark side not very appealing. A small piece of grease had caught fire and dripped through the bottom of the grill, landing on the dry grass. Immediately it burst into flames. I frantically shut the lid, turned off the propane, and moved the grill away, fearing our new BBQ might catch fire. How would I explain that to Julie?

I quickly found that stomping wildly with my flip-flops spread the fire even more. I looked around frantically for a Pulaski or any such tool, but there was nothing nearby to fight the fire.

A vision of the headlines in the local paper came to mind: **Krassel firefighter burns down ranger's house in downtown New Meadows while on break from fighting fire!**

Another thing I didn't want to have to explain to Julie.

Panic set in. I looked over at the faucet on the side of the house. No hose was attached. There was a hose on the other faucet at the front of the house, but it wouldn't reach this far. I grabbed a shovel from the garage and hit the grass. The fire would appear to go out for a moment, then burst back into flames. I had to do something fast.

Finally, I grabbed an old coat from the mudroom and soaked it with water from the faucet on the side of the house. Soon I was sweaty and black, but the fire was out. Unfortunately, the steak wasn't edible, completely burnt through on one side. I opened a can of chili and poured it over the potato.

Have you ever had a week like that? Dan, a good buddy of mine, called the other day. We got to talking about retirement. I asked him when he was going to retire.

Dan just laughed. He said, "I thought we might retire in a couple of years, but it seems like every time we get a little ahead, something comes by and knocks us back down. That seems to be happening my whole life, why do you think that is, Bill?" he asked.

That was a very good question. After hanging up, I thought about it for a while. I think I finally have an idea.

First, life is hard. Nowhere in the Bible does it say that it will be easy. That stems from the fall in the garden with Adam and Eve. Because of that, we all will suffer.

It says in Genesis 3:17-19, *Then to Adam He said, "Because you have heeded the voice of your wife, and have eaten from the tree of which I commanded you, saying, 'You shall not eat of it.'"*

"Cursed is the ground for your sake; In toil, you shall eat of it
all the days of your life. Both thorns and thistles it shall bring forth for you, and you shall eat the herb of the field.
In the sweat of your face, you shall eat bread
Till you return to the ground."

So there you go. We plug away, trying to get ahead so we can enjoy life. And then something unexpected comes along and pulls the rug out from under us, and here we sit, knocked back on our butt again.

For the longest time, I didn't think that I needed God. I was young and strong. I was a self-made man, or so I thought. Although I still had a little faith, I believed if I worked hard,, God would bless me. However, I wasn't going to put much effort into talking to someone I couldn't see. Praying to Jesus was a little too much for me. I didn't want to be one of *those* folks. You know, the ones who were always hounding you to have a personal relationship with Jesus.

I rebelled against that kind of relationship. When I spoke with God, it was going to be on my terms, up in the mountains, fishing in a stream. And honestly, that is where God met me. Inadvertently I would ask Him, without even realizing, some of the deeper questions in life. He was patient with me. He answered through circumstances in life itself. The problem was, I wasn't paying attention.

As I plugged along, I began to see that pattern of failure Dan had been talking about. I could count on it; every time I got ahead, something unexpected happened to knock me back. I began to see that I wasn't the one in control, no matter how self-sufficient I thought I was or how hard I tried.

What if there was something with this whole Jesus thing? It would be kind of shallow on my part to not at least ask. Wouldn't it? I mean, surely, being a self-made man, I could decipher whether this Jesus thing was a bunch of hooey, couldn't I? Ultimately, it was my decision anyway, nobody else's. I could ask Jesus about it, and no one would even have to know, right? So that is what I did.

It was in July 1996, after a hard fall off a neighbor's roof, I couldn't stand up because I had shattered my heel. I got fed up with this game and asked the question that had been nagging at me ever since the grizzly encounter.

I said, "Jesus, I don't know you, but I have heard about you. I need help."

I didn't have to say anything more. No special prayer or anything, He knew me better than I knew myself. Shoot, he had been trying to get my attention for years. I wasn't paying attention or was too proud to accept it.

That painful fall was the one that got me on my knees. Jesus met me there on the floor in Darby, Montana, July 28, 1996, at 4:28 A.M. He answered, and then it was my turn to respond. I could deny it and say this wasn't real, or I would have to admit it for what it was. The only thing I had to do was be honest with myself. That's what we all have to do, isn't it?

God is pretty patient with us. If you are as stubborn as I was eventually His patience runs thin and He gets your attention the hard way. Just sayin, don't wait til He kicks you off the roof. I suspect that stirring in your gut is telling you to act.

Authority

Joshua 1:9

Have I not commanded you? Be strong and courageous. Do not be terrified; do not be discouraged, for the Lord your God will be with you wherever you go."

A white flick of a tail caught my eye as I removed the load straps securing the Yamaha 175 in the back of the truck. Across the road, a small whitetail buck finished checking me out and continued with his day. It was a brisk morning, one of the first heavy frosts of fall on the Sula district, in the remote backcountry of southwestern Montana.

The frost made me wonder when the deer's coats would begin changing from summer to winter. The little buck's reddish-brown summer coat stood out in contrast to the frosty morning, where the lighter gray winter coat would blend in. The little three-point had rubbed most of the velvet from his antlers, so I surmised he was probably in the transition stage of changing to his gray winter coat. A white puff of breath escaped sharply from his nostrils as he blew a warning about my presence to other deer in the area. I attached the Forest Service radio to my belt, stowed the camera and metal clipboard in my backpack, and bungee-strapped the pack to the bike. As I did so, I thought about what a great job I had. My supervisor encouraged me to work whatever hours I wanted, as long as the

Watershed Improvement Needs survey got done. I preferred getting to work early so I could be on the mountain before the sun came up. My personal mission on this job was to scout for elk. The elk had just started bugling. I had a bugle and a cow call tucked in my pack for easy access, along with maps specifically showing elk and deer hotspots.

That summer, the entire Bitterroot National Forest was being surveyed for various sources of sediment deposition in the Bitterroot River drainage. Sediment was the culprit blamed for plugging threatened cutthroat trout spawning redds. One of the primary areas of concern were old logging roads built in the early 1930s and 40s when they used logs as culverts for stream crossings. After all these years the simple manmade culverts were starting to decompose and fail, contributing large concentrations of granitic soil flushing downstream through the watershed. My job, a seasonal appointment, was to identify these sources and write a rehab plan for the District before they all started failing. My fieldwork for the summer was winding down. The Sula District was one of the more remote historical logging areas left on the survey.

The first old logging road I encountered that morning had started out open, but soon the brush became heavy enough to hamper a four-wheeler. My motorcycle made it through easily. I had ridden up the obscure road about a mile when it crossed over to the northeastern aspect which was dense with brush. Alder several inches in diameter grew up thick and high from the cut bank and curved upwards into the road. It became easier to walk than ride, so I decided at the next wide spot I would stop the bike and walk the rest of the road out. With the motorcycle, I pushed through an exceptionally overgrown section of alder to an opening of about 40 yards.

At the edge of the opening, I noticed a dead mule deer buck covered in leaves. I stopped the bike to get a closer look. It had a small forked horn, but what caught my eye was its gray winter coat. Because it was covered with leaves, I knew immediately it was a mountain-lion kill.

Prior to moving to Montana, I had worked on the South Fork of the Salmon River Corridor doing predator surveys. This kill was intriguing to me, and I wanted to take some photos to add to my library of various predator kills.

I shut off the motorcycle and pulled the camera from the pack. Kneeling next to the small buck, I grabbed hold of one of the hind legs and moved it to see if rigor mortis had set in yet. The leg moved freely. Steam immediately rose from the carcass. The deer's eyes were still clear. A portion of the hindquarters had been freshly eaten on. I laid my hand on the dead animal and noted it was warm. This was a really fresh kill.

Suddenly I heard a noise about fifteen feet behind me in the brush. I turned, and through the heavy brush, I made out a reddish-brown section of an animal. I could only make out the contrasting light area where the tail and the hindquarters joined. It looked similar to the small whitetail I had seen when I was unloading the motorcycle. I thought, *what in the world is a whitetail doing this close to a mountain-lion kill?*

When the animal flicked its long tail, I realized the trouble I was in. I stood up slowly to make myself as large as possible and took a step to the side to see around a tree which was blocking the view of its head. My heart sank when my eyes met the giant cat's eyes. Its ears were laid back flat against its head, and its eyes were dilated, almost entirely black. When our eyes met, its tail began to whip anxiously. I knew better than to lose eye contact. *This was going to be the granddaddy of staring contests.* My mind raced to figure out what to do. The bike was facing the cat, and it would take some maneuvering to turn it around in this brush. I had no gun nor any other protection. Most worrisome, I was trying to force a mountain lion off his own kill.

Taking a step towards the angry cat, I said, "Get out of here!" in as deep of voice as I could. My legs shook uncontrollably. I desperately hoped the cat couldn't sense how scared I was.

The cat stopped my advance abruptly with a deep, drawn-out growl followed by an intense hiss.

Oh, man, this is such a bad predicament, I thought. *Maybe I could spook it off if I threw something at it.* I didn't dare to take my eyes off the cat to see if there was anything close by to throw. Then I realized the camera was in my hand. I had one shot.

I raised my arm to throw the camera as hard as I could when Sula Peak Lookout called in for a fire check. As the radio's squelch sounded, the big cat's eyes shifted from mine for a split second.

That gave me an idea. I turned up the squelch on the radio and took another step towards the animal. This time the giant cat took his eyes off me nervously, then glanced back. I took another step towards the angry feline. He slowly sat up, looking nervously around. With the next step, he reluctantly turned away, walked several feet, and turned back, facing me and growling another weak warning. I said in a firm, low voice, "Get out of here!"

He growled again at me, and with some serious stink eye, he disappeared up the road. A sense of relief rushed through me, but there was still a problem. I needed to continue up the same logging road he had just walked up.

After taking a few quick photos of the kill, I started the motorcycle and continued up the road to finish my surveying work. It unnerved me when I had to ride back past the kill. I half expected the cat to jump on me on my way back through.

I liken this experience with the lion to we humans and the spiritual world. Since the fall of man with Adam and Eve in the garden, this world has been under the dominion of Satan. There are times when we run smack dab into one of his little demons. Most people are not aware of it, but there is a constant spiritual battle being waged all around us, behind the scenes in the spiritual realm. It truly is a battle between good and evil.

Ephesians 6:12 *"For **we do not wrestle** against flesh and blood, but against principalities, against powers, against the rulers of the darkness of this age, against spiritual hosts of wickedness in the heavenly places"*

I didn't understand this until after I became a Christian, but the name of Jesus works very similar to how the squelch of that radio worked. There is nothing stronger than the name of Jesus. The entire spiritual world is under the authority of Jesus. Remember in the last chapter, when I explained how Jesus indwells you? He has also given you the authority to use His name, Jesus.

The next time you feel an attack of fear penetrating your mind, take authority over it with the name of Jesus. If you are His child, He has given you that authority. Use it, and the demons tormenting you will turn away faster than that cat did!

Winter Camping

Psalm 34:7

"The angel of the Lord encamps around those who fear Him, and He delivers them."

It had been a long day bow-hunting for elk. The mountains in southwestern Montana had been dumped on with early snow in the last week of September. My hunting partner, Steve, and I had been chasing a bull around Pioneer Lake for most of the afternoon.

Visions of the big bull replayed through my mind. Each time I closed my eyes, I could see the big bull with his giant rack raking the ten-foot lodgepole pine to shreds. The whole mountain had shaken when he turned to bugle at us. That echo from the mountain amphitheater around the lake stuck in my mind.

I was wet and exhausted when I stopped by the Pump and Pak convenient store. A hot shot of coffee before heading to the farm was just an excuse for stopping. The real reason was Anna's car was parked outside. I didn't need a jolt of caffeine, either. Seeing Anna's car parked out back sent a shot of something that erased all the exhaustion in my body. I used any excuse to stop in when Anna was working. I knew her from an algebra class I was struggling with at Montana State University. Truth be told, the primary reason for struggling in the algebra class was the distraction of fishing and archery season.

"You were not in class today," Anna chided when I walked in the door. I ignored her and headed to the coffee. Returning to the cash register, I waited patiently until the customer she was waiting on had left.

When the bell on the door clanged behind him, I excitedly told Anna about the giant bull. She listened earnestly while I reenacted how the bull had eluded us all day. I expressed how I wanted to go back up and spend the night at the lake to see if I could get him.

"You're going up and camping in all of this snow this time of year?" she exclaimed in surprise.

"Of course! There's only ten or so inches up there. Besides, the snow keeps the bugs away."

"Don't you freeze at night?" she asked.

"No, I have a good sleeping bag," I replied confidently.

Anna studied me intently as I took a big sip of coffee. "I have always wanted to go winter camping, but I don't like to get cold," she said, folding her arms tightly.

"Why don't you come with me tomorrow? We don't have school." I said. "It's only a mile in there, and I will cook dinner for you. How can you beat an offer like that?"

Anna was thinking about it when a customer came in to buy a can of Copenhagen and a six-pack of beer. After the customer left, she shocked me when she agreed, if her coworker Darcie would cover her shift.

"Bill, do you promise to protect me?"

"Of course!" I said. "You will be in the best care possible."

Anna quickly called Darcie. I heard her say, "Yes, the guy who works at Bozeman Brick. He asked me to go winter camping tomorrow, but I have to work tomorrow night. Will you cover for me?"

Anna was quite excited, but apparently her friend showed concern. I could only hear one side of the conversation, but it was clear her friend was asking a lot of questions. I heard Anna say, "I know, but this guy is harmless. Please!"

Her friend obviously agreed to cover Anna's shift. Anna turned and smiled at me, nodding.

I was more than shocked by her answer because I was completely bluffing it. I had been working up the courage to ask Anna out for a couple of months. Now the pressure was on! I needed to come up with a pretty spectacular meal cooked over a fire.

I told her what to bring for clothes, and that she could use an extra sleeping bag I had that was good to -10 degrees. Her friend had a backpack she could use, and after growing up in North Dakota, she knew how to layer up on clothes to keep warm.

The next day I stopped by Anna's apartment to pick her up. She looked so darn cute with those dark brown curls shooting out from her wool hat. She seemed adequately prepared with a wool sweater and pants, and Sorel boots. I helped Anna attach the sleeping pad and bag onto her backpack, and we were ready to head out of town.

The higher we climbed, the deeper the snow became. The tracks Steve and I had made the day before were filled in, but we could see them, which made the drive up the mountain a little less ominous. I got out once, with an excuse to go to the bathroom, but it was more to check out the depth of the heavy snow. The front differential was pushing snow, but the truck was having no problems busting through it. The last thing I wanted was to get snowed in at the top. At least it was all downhill if we could just get to the overlook. Our fresh tracks would help show us the way back down the mountain, unless we got dumped on. Snow was still falling in flakes as large as chicken feathers. The forecast had called for the snow to slow overnight and clear by morning A clear sky would mean a cold night, but we'd also have a chance to see the animals that would come out to feed when the snow tapered off.

When we reached the summit and got out of the truck, I could tell Anna was anxious. She was standing in a good foot of snow, smiling nervously, with her hands in her pockets. Large flakes contrasted against her dark brown curls.

"Are you sure you have done this before? This is kind of crazy!" There was an ever-so-slight hesitation in her voice.

I laughed. "It's going to be just fine. Trust me!"

I don't know why I thought those words would sound good. If anyone ever said that to me, I'd have backed up like a government mule.

Anna didn't know me very well. Serious second thoughts edged into her mind. After all, I was just some guy who stopped in where she worked, with a nice smile, who made her laugh occasionally. Now she was alone with me on top of this mountain, in what appeared to be a few flakes short of a blizzard, ready to descend into the wilderness to a lake she couldn't see. Before she could back out, I quickly grabbed my backpack and bow. "C'mon, we need to get going before it gets dark."

She scrambled to get her pack on for fear of being left alone at the truck. She seemed on the verge of panic. I helped her get her pack on, gave her my walking stick, and looked into her big brown eyes.

"It's going to be okay, Anna. I promise."

She smiled sheepishly. then looked nervously to the ground. She still was not completely convinced, and maybe nervous that I was able to read her mind.

Typically, I would have slipped quietly unannounced into the secret lair of the bull elk I was hunting. With Anna's uneasiness, I figured I'd better forget about hunting for the big bull and settle on a pleasant winter camping experience. Anna's creased brow showed a touch of fear, and I did my best to quench it.

On the way down, I quietly explained to Anna where we had previously seen the bull. I am not sure if it helped to stop on top of a ridge and show her where we were going to camp, since it was completely socked in with heavy clouds. The little lake probably froze solid over the winter, so didn't contain fish. Nonetheless, it was a beautiful lake surrounded by a grassy meadow on one side and a granite outcropping on the other.

We cut the giant bull's track three-quarters of the way down to the lake. The tracks were old and had plenty of snow in them. They'd probably been made that morning when he side hilled above the lake to the meadow to feed.

I was pretty sure we were in the bull's earshot, so I signaled to Anna to be quiet while fumbling for my bugle. I let out a bugle followed by a couple of squeals. The big bull answered immediately, from a deep patch of timber somewhere way below the lake. His reply sounded like it came out of a 55-gallon barrel, deep and coarse. The squeals that followed echoed through the basin below. I was surprised he answered, with as much noise as we had been making up until then.

Anna's fear of being alone in the woods with me disappeared quickly. Now I was an asset, the animal who had just answered had her complete attention.

After a few minutes, I let out another bugle. This time the bull didn't answer. He was playing his game, just like he did the previous afternoon with Steve and me.

The overall hike was not steep, and within an hour we reached our destination. We set up the tent in a small clearing at one end of the lake, where the meadow dropped off into the dark timber where the bull had answered.

I assigned Anna to firewood-gathering detail while I set up the tent. She stuck close to camp in her search. I caught her more than once gazing off in the direction of where the bull had bugled.

Pickings were slim for firewood in a foot of snow. Most of the dryer wood were dead branches that needed to be broken off the trees. After I had the tent set up, I gave her a hand. Before long, we had a large pile of firewood that would last the night. It was a beautiful camp with a lakeside view. Anna seemed quite impressed and huddled close to the blazing fire.

Near the fire sat a small boulder which I used for a table to prepare the meal. I had packed the bread in a coffee tin so it wouldn't get smashed, then used the tin to boil water over the fire. I sliced the carrots and potatoes into strips, put them in a cooking bag, and poured half the boiling water into the bag with them. Then I put the cooking bag into the coffee tin and set it back on the fire to cook. The coffee tin was equipped with a wire bail-type handle to pick it up and move it easily from over the fire. Coals on one side of the fire had burned down to blazing-hot orange, ready to grill the meat. While the steaks were cooking, I sliced mushrooms, onions, and green peppers, and sautéed them with butter in the frying pan. After the potatoes and onions had boiled for ten minutes or so, I drained the water and added them to the skillet with the mushrooms and onions, and seasoned it with salt, pepper, basil and a little garlic powder. The combined aroma of the vegetables and the steaks brightened Anna's spirits. She all but forgot about the bull elk that had bugled earlier.

With the meal served on paper plates, I restoked the fire to boil water in the coffee tin for hot chocolate later. Anna was full of questions, absorbing every move.

After dinner, we sipped hot chocolate and got to know each other. Winter camping was daunting to her. She confessed that her idea of roughing it was a camp trailer in a paved parking spot with a black-and-white T.V. This trip was a true wilderness experience for her.

The orange glow from the campfire flickered between the two of us and beyond as it faded into the serene stillness of the snowy Montana night. Our voices and occasional laughter gently echoed across the lake before being absorbed by the darkness.

Eventually the subject changed to bears. She was curious whether I had ever run into any when I was camping. Against my better judgment, I told her the story of the grizzly that had come up behind the tent. Her eyes grew wide as I described the clacking teeth and the way the bear ran off down the hill. Feeding off her interest in the subject, I shared another story about when Steve and I were hunting elk up the canyon in the Portal Creek drainage.

I explained how I'd heard that a lake called Hidden Lake contained golden trout. Steve and I brought along our fishing poles, planning to fish there before scouting elk. Steve had stayed out a little too late the night before, so when we reached the lake, he took a nap while I fished. I put a black gnat on my line, and the small golden trout were hitting well. As I worked my way around the lake, I noticed large rocks that had been upturned. I speculated whatever was flipping these rocks over had to be good sized. Halfway around the lake, it occurred to me that it might be a grizzly turning over all those rocks, looking for grubs. Some of the rocks were huge. The freshness of the sign and this sudden realization put a damper on fishing. I figured it was a great time to switch our pursuit to elk. I mentioned to Steve the grizzly sign on the other side of the lake, and he agreed that it was a good time to head in the opposite direction.

We cut down the mountain towards some open parks along the ridge to see if we could locate any fresh elk activity. To get there, we had to work through a thick stand of lodgepole pine. Residual patches of snow from an earlier snowstorm dotted the cooler northern slopes. We had not been hiking very long when we jumped something ahead of us. It crashed through the heavy timber a short way, then stopped.

Steve and I each knocked an arrow in our bow and quietly headed in the direction of the noise. Each step was gingerly placed to not make a sound. We scarcely breathed, our hearts racing with anticipation. Suddenly Steve's hand shot up to stop me. He pointed ahead. A cow moose with a calf stood thirty yards ahead of us. Her ears switched back and forth as she lifted her nose to catch our scent. I felt the downslope winds shift in her favor. It seemed to take forever for the scent to carry to her, but when it met her nostrils, both animals bolted and headed down the mountain, crashing through the brush.

Anna jumped when something popped in the timber below the lake, bringing our thoughts back to the present. She moved to my side of the fire as we looked in the direction of the pop.

"So, what happened with the moose?" she asked.

Staring into the fire, I went on with the story. "We continued along towards the open parks over the next ridge. We hadn't gone far when we came to a small spring with fresh water running down the mountain. We were both thirsty and decided to get a drink from the spring. Getting down on all fours, I bent to get a drink when I noticed sediment swirling in the water. "Something just walked through here." I said.

"That cow and calf must have circled and gotten around ahead of us." Steve said as he too bent down to drink.

I stood and looked for tracks in the small snowdrift on the other side of the small spring. There in the wet snow was a very fresh, large grizzly track. I made a track in the snow next to it and pulled my foot back. The large claws extended beyond my boot track, making my stomach turn sour. Suddenly, looking for elk seemed less appealing. With minimal discussion, we adjusted our trajectory towards the truck.

Anna hung onto every word of the story all the way to the end. With the story over, she shifted nervously every now and then, casting a glance towards the spot from where the noise had previously come.

Leaving Anna at the safety of the fire, I broke away from camp to the edge of the flickering light to relieve myself. The temperature was dropping, which meant the clouds had cleared. The stars took my breath away as they lit up the Montana sky in a brilliant display of light. The Milky Way stretched from one side of the horizon to the other. There were so many stars, at first the cluster looked to be a cloud, until closer inspection.

Back at the fire, Anna was brushing her teeth. When she finished, I encouraged her to go with me to the edge of the fire's light to look at the stars. She gazed at the stars, although seemed preoccupied with something else. She looked and listened intently, but her focus was into the darkness beyond where we were standing. I realized she probably had to go to the bathroom, and might be scared, so I asked if she wanted me to go with her. I offered to stand on the other side of the tree. Gauging her reaction, we still didn't know each other well enough, so I left her there and went back to the light of the fire to brush my teeth, clean up, and put things away for the night. When Anna returned, her face shone bright with a sense of accomplishment.

It didn't hit me until we both got into the tent next to each other. This was the closest I had ever been to Anna. Nervousness swept over me. Should I kiss her good night? Oh, man, this was so out of my comfort zone. I figured it was best to play it safe and wait until a better time to do something like that.

After we had crawled into our sleeping bags and gotten settled in, Anna confessed she had never slept in a tent on the ground before. I told her it was exactly like sleeping in a bed except a little harder, and by morning, there would be one small rock or pinecone she'd had to avoid all night. I explained that I couldn't sleep in my clothes because they bunched up, making for a long and miserable night. Undressing down to my long underwear bottoms inside my sleeping bag, I explained how I used my clothes for a pillow. My ingenuity didn't seem to impress her. She had brought a pillow.

I had to wonder what she thought as I undressed next to her. She opted to sleep in all her clothes. I wondered whether she would get any sleep at all. I was exhausted and told Anna if I happen to snore, she should nudge me and I would change my position. I was asleep before my head hit my homemade pillow.

Somewhere in the middle of the night, I was awakened by a direct "Psssst!" accompanied by a sharp elbow in the ribs.

Suddenly it seemed as though we had been married for quite some time.

"What?" I said sleepily, "Was I snoring?"

"Noooo! Something's out there! LISTEN!" she said sternly.

When someone says, "Something is out there!" in the middle of the night and you're somewhere in the backcountry of Montana, it is going to take a little while before you get your heart rate down enough to hear anything. Between the heartbeat pounding in my ear and the rustling of the sleeping bag next to me, I couldn't hear a thing.

" What is it?" she stammered impatiently.

I whispered sharply, "Shhhh..."

We both held our breath for about a minute. Then I heard what she was talking about. Something was walking along the lake. Occasionally I could hear a thump and a splash in the water. Then I heard the creature pull up grass and eat it noisily.

"It's a bear!" she hissed, snuggling a little closer to me. Her voice was quivering. She was on the verge of panic. Visions of my childhood with Monica flashed through my mind. I resisted the urge to dive to the bottom of my sleeping bag and assume the fetal position.

Continuing to listen closely, I heard the clunk of a hoof hitting a log as the animal stepped over it.

I slowly unzipped the fly to the tent. As quietly as I could, I pulled the covers of my sleeping bag back. I grabbed the bow lying next to me and started to wriggle myself out.

Instantly I felt a firm grip on my arm accompanied with a direct whisper in my ear. Something like claws dug sharply into my skin. "Where are *you* going?" she demanded.

The animal was walking up the shoreline towards our tent. It wouldn't be long before it passed by. With all the talking, it had stopped. I didn't want to spook it off.

"I want to see what it is," I whispered.

I knocked an arrow just in case it was something other than what I presumed. Anna mumbled under her breath, "Oh, great, we're going to die."

I started laughing and was having a hard time holding it in.

"We're not going to die," I said.

The front half of my body was out of the tent. The cool air felt good on my bare skin. I was holding my breath, trying to be as quiet as I could.

I could hear Anna murmuring something under her breath. Something like "Dear Heavenly Father, something, something ... please Lord, cover us with the blood of Jesus." and then it was quiet. Anna was holding her breath, expecting any second a grizzly would engulf the tent and kill me, leaving her to hike out of this dreadful wilderness alone.

I couldn't quite see around the tent enough to catch a glimpse of the animal. It had stopped making noise. I assumed it was listening to us. Another few inches and I would be clear. I had the arrow knocked, with a little tension on the string of the recurve bow to keep the arrow from falling out of place.

I reached out for one more skootch when, without warning, Whoomph! The whole tent collapsed on top of us. Anna let out a blood-curdling scream and began thrashing violently inside the fallen tent. All the commotion caused me to jump releasing the tension on the arrow, sending it into the lake. The big bull whirled around and disappeared back into the dark timber.

I started laughing when I realized what had happened. A large clump of wet snow had fallen out of the tree and landed squarely on top of the tent, collapsing it.

Anna was almost crying. Since I was halfway out of the tent, I slipped my Sorels on and set the tent back up.

The next morning, we walked the shoreline. The big bull had walked within thirty yards of the tent. The aluminum arrow was stuck twenty feet out in the shallow lake.

It goes to show you how a little talk can plant ideas in your mind and, once planted, can grow those little fears into large fears, which happens to be one of Satan's best scare tactics. Much of the time, what we fear doesn't even come to pass. It is nothing more than a bunch of "what ifs."

I learned a few things from this experience. One is, be careful telling bear stories before you hit the sack in the mountains. The other is, our God has a very good sense of humor. One of the greatest gifts He has given us is the gift of laughter. It can diffuse fear from a tense situation. An even greater gift He has given us is the gift of prayer. Anna was so scared she turned to God for help, and God answered, just not in the way she thought He would. Most people wait around, relying on what they can do in their own strength before calling on the Lord.

I think the Lord enjoyed that night. I imagine Him with a handful of angels watching. "Hey, watch this! Oh, this is going to be good!" as He flicked that little chunk of snow out of the tree, right smack on top of the tent.

Have you ever seen God's sense of humor?

The Mountain Car

Romans 8:38-39

"For I am persuaded that neither death nor life, nor angels nor principalities nor powers, nor things present nor things to come, nor height nor depth, nor any other created thing shall be able to separate us from the love of God which is in Christ Jesus our Lord"

As I put the last screw in the drywall, I heard Merl's "one bark" warning. Someone had pulled up in the driveway. Merl was my Australian Shepherd. He was a very social dog and head of the greeting committee there at the farm. He usually barked once to let me know when someone was driving down the driveway before heading out to his self-assigned position.

I set the screw gun down and removed my carpenter's apron before heading out to the driveway to see who it might be. I wasn't expecting anyone and was surprised to see a tall, slender woman get out of a early-90's Subaru. She was accompanied by a young lady around the age of 15 whom I assumed to be her daughter. Both ladies were wearing shorts on this fine summer morning. The sun was bright, and I squinted to see them clearly.

"Hello there," the woman said.

When I heard her voice, I recognized who she was. I had shown Karen property earlier in the week. She was a single mom with apparently three daughters. The oldest one was with her today.

Karen was recently divorced and currently living just south of Missoula. She was interested in purchasing a small place in the Bitterroot Valley and was looking around Darby. I had shown her the few properties I was aware of. We had a good time while we were looking, and she had mentioned that she might be back over the weekend.

I had assumed she would call if she was going to come down to Darby. Obviously, she hadn't. She said she had stopped by the realty office and Don, my broker, had tried to call but when no one answered, he sent her to my house.

After some small talk, she asked me what I was working on and, looking over my shoulder, hinted she wanted a tour of the house. I took the hint and led the way to the drywall project I had just finished in the bathroom.

The three of us all crowded into the bathroom. Karen touched a lot when she spoke. The little bathroom seemed to get smaller as we ran out of things to talk about, I began to feel claustrophobic, with a dire need for fresh air. The problem was, I was the furthest one in the bathroom, and there was not enough room to pass the women in a tactful way. I thought fast and came up a good excuse to move along: iced tea. Fortunately, everyone was thirsty and Karen's daughter, Kristen, led the way out of the confined room back to the open deck outside.

A gentle breeze carried the scent of the pine trees off the hill across from the deck, lifting the napkins under our glasses. We discussed some of the properties we had looked at the previous day and potential lending options. At a slow point in the conversation, Kristen spoke up, asking, "Mom said you had a car you might be interested in selling."

"Oh, yeah, the Mountain Car," I said excitedly. "Do you know why I call it the Mountain Car?"

The young lady shook her head shyly.

"Well, when I worked for the Forest Service over in Idaho, I needed a car with good gas mileage. It would've cost me a small fortune to drive that old three-quarter-ton Ford back and forth. In Idaho, I worked at the edge of the Frank Church Wilderness Area at a workstation called Elk Creek Guard Station. It was located in the headwaters of the Salmon River. After work, I used to take the car around the meadows in Bear Valley to spot and photograph elk. Everyone on the crew called it the Mountain Car and, well, I guess the name stuck."

Kristen listened politely while I continued.

"I bought the Mountain Car from my Uncle Larry over in Colton, Washington. He used it to store grain for his horses. It smelled like mice when I got it, so I had to drive it with the windows rolled down most of the time."

Kristen's eyebrows went up. I knew what she was thinking, so I said. "It doesn't smell like that too much anymore. I think most of the mice fell out after the first couple of trips to Idaho. The back roads had a lot of washboards on them."

"Oh," Kristen responded, nervously looking at me and then at her mom.

I continued with the sales pitch. "It's a 1986 Subaru, and I think it has probably a hundred and eighty-six thousand miles on it. It uses a little oil, but I have never had a problem with it. I would sell it to you for what I bought it for. I paid $300 for it."

"That's a pretty good price, Bill. Are you sure?" Karen interjected.

"Well, take a look at it. It's got a few miles, but it's a dependable car," I replied.

Karen and Kristen looked at each other and shrugged.

Kristen then looked back at me, and I asked, "Do you want to take it for a spin?"

Kristen responded with a definite "Sure!"

I asked Kristen if she had been driving long and Karen interjected, saying, "She has been driving my car with me alongside now for about a year. I think she is ready for a car of her own now." Kristen beamed proudly at her mom, and at the announcement she would be graduating to a car of her own.

"Oh, shoot, it's a stick shift," I suddenly remembered. "Have you ever driven a stick shift?"

We stopped in the middle of the gravel driveway. Kristen's bright smile went dull. "No, I haven't." She looked at her mom, heartbroken.

"Oh, don't worry about it. I'll teach you," I said confidently, which brought half of her smile back. Yet she was still nervously reserved.

I had parked the Mountain Car behind the house in front of the red board-and-batten shed next to the smokehouse. I hadn't started it over the winter, and honestly wasn't sure if it would even turn over.

Climbing into the driver's seat, I pumped the gas pedal once and turned the key over. The trusty old Mountain Car fired right up.

Both girls squealed with delight. Kristen looked like she was envisioning driving the Mountain Car to school, her friends in the back seat with the music cranked.

After double-checking to make sure the car was in neutral, I set the emergency brake, shut off the engine, and hopped out, motioning for Kristen to get in.

From the passenger's seat, I explained to her how to push the clutch in and start the car. She was understandably nervous, and I patiently showed her where the gears were.

I said, "Let's just start off in first and go around the house and down the driveway before we try shifting, okay?

Kristen nodded firmly, her blue eyes bright and alert.

"Now put it in first gear and slowly let out the clutch while you give it a little gas," I said softly.

She let out the clutch, and the car died. Kristen apologized, and I said, "It's okay, just give it a little more gas as you let out the clutch."

Karen was standing off to the side, cheering Kirsten on. The car was facing the back of the house. Kristen started the car again and gave it a little more gas. The car lurched forward and died again.

Kristen sighed deeply, becoming frustrated. I double-checked to make sure she was in first gear and said. "That's okay. Just give it a little more gas and I think you'll have it."

Kristen was ready to give up. I felt her pain. To put her at ease, I said, "I think the registration is still here in the glove box." I reached to open it.

Kristen had started the car for the third time. As instructed, she gave it a lot more gas while dumping the clutch. The Mountain Car lurched forward, lunging back and forth wildly, just as the glove box opened.

Without warning, a giant pack rat leaped out of the glove compartment and landed squarely in my lap. I gasped loudly and brushed the furry varmint to the floorboard in sheer panic. The gray creature with its long, hairy tail scurried for safety, finding the open leg to my bib overalls a perfect place to escape. It proceeded to climb up the leg of my overalls, while I frantically blocked its advance with my right boot. With adrenaline on my side, the boot sufficiently blocked the rat's advance just below my knee. The rat was reluctantly persuaded to release its death grip on the overall material. The sensation of the furry creature against the bare skin of my leg pushed me to the edge of pandemonium, just shy of screaming like a girl. The alien creature abruptly changed direction, opting for another escape route. With much stomping, I was able to securely pin him against the floor of the car before he went up the other pant leg.

In the meantime, in shock over the drama unfolding next to her, Kristen floored the gas pedal in horror. I looked up and realized we were speeding straight toward the back of the house. Merl dove for cover under the porch.

I reached over, grabbed the steering wheel, and pulled it hard to the right, barely missing the corner of the house. The car slid sideways across the lawn and on down to the end of the lane before Kristen regained her composure.

The packrat was pinned to the floor with my foot. Its back legs worked frantically on the floorboards. There was no way I was going to let up on the pressure. Kristen's focus was directed on the packrat much more than on driving at this point. As calmly as I could, I suggested letting off the gas and turning around at the end of the lane. When we got back to the house, Karen was standing there aghast. "What in the world happened?" she asked.

Kristen couldn't wait to get out of the car. She didn't bother to shut the engine off. Fortunately, I slipped the car in neutral and pulled up the emergency brake.

"Oh, Mom, you wouldn't believe it! That was the biggest rat I have ever seen!" Karen consoled her daughter on the way back to their car, and they left.

They didn't buy the car, and, well, they never visited again, either.

That's just how it works. You are working along, minding your own business, doing whatever you need to get done in life. Suddenly, an opportunity arises for you to bless someone, and Satan and his little minions jump in your lap to get your eyes off-track. If he can distract you, he will. He will do his best to get you to take your eyes off the Lord and put them on your circumstances and everything going on around you.

Isn't that what happened to Peter when he stepped out of the boat? He saw the Lord walking on water and headed straight towards him, completely focused on his Lord. As long as Peter had his eyes focused on the Lord, he was fine. The storm that night was tumultuous, but Peter didn't falter until he began focusing on the waves around him.

When Satan's little demons dump something in your lap to distract you, brush them to the floor and step on their heads. You have been given the power. He has no jurisdiction over you as long as you're a child of God. Focus on the Lord and keep walking down the path. There is nothing that can separate you from the love of the Lord.

Inner Walls

Isaiah 61:1

"The Spirit of the LORD GOD is on me, because the Lord has anointed me to preach good tidings to the poor. He has sent me to heal the brokenhearted, proclaim liberty to the captives, and the opening to the prison, to those who are bound."

"One more, Tim, for the both of us," Carl said, "then I better head home."

"Okay," Tim replied as he poured two draft beers.

"Oh, before I forget, I need a bear tag too." Carl added. "That bear got into my refrigerator again last night and ate my lunch. I had to go hungry today."

"And you know how grumpy Carl gets when he doesn't eat," I said. "He was a bear today!"

"That dang bear is getting pretty gutsy anymore. I went home last night, and there were paw prints on my windows." Carl responded.

"That's not good," I said, "You better cure that problem before you have to buy a new window!"

Carl and I finished up our pool game and headed home for the night. He looked like he might have had a little too much to drink, so I offered to give him a ride home. Like that would have been any safer!

"No, I got it," he said, "But thanks!" With one kick, his Harley responded with a thundering roar.

I was concerned about Carl. His remote one-bedroom cabin sat several miles down Cougar Creek, nestled along the backside of the meadow. It was a Friday and we had stayed out late playing pool at Tim's. There would be no traffic on the dirt back road at one o'clock in the morning. The road wove five miles through a myriad of dark timber and clear-cuts just above the meadow. *He'll be okay,* I thought. *That Harley makes so much racket that if the noise doesn't warn the wildlife, the vibration will.*

As he told me later, Carl rode the Harley down the back road, weaving back and forth, trying to keep his balance. He probably didn't need those last two beers. It was difficult to focus with both eyes, so he tried driving with just one. That helped some, but his depth perception was off just a bit. The odds of meeting anyone on that dirt road that late at night was slim, and if he did, they'd most likely be lost. He had to worry more about running into a moose than into another rig. Moose were black, thus hard to see in the dark, and slow to move sometimes.

The rough driveway to Carl's cabin was more of a skid trail than a driveway. As he drove up, he half expected to catch a bear inside the one-room cabin. He used the light on the bike to scour the surrounding area. At one point he saw a dark flash just off the road. Turning the motorcycle sharply to catch a look with the headlight caused him to lose his balance. *Phew, that was close! I need to get to bed*, he thought.

Carl stopped the bike in front of the one-room log cabin, headlight shining on the front door. He revved the bike loudly several times to spook anything that might be lingering in the woods around the cabin. He made note of anything he might trip over on the way to the door before shutting the light off. The contents of his refrigerator, nothing more than a red cooler which normally sat on the front step of his cabin, had been dispersed across the ground. The lid bore teeth marks in one corner.

"Dang bear!" he mumbled as he kicked the red cooler out of the way. He fumbled to unlock the padlock in the dark and jumped when Fang, his bob-tailed cat, leapt out of the tree, landing next to him.

"Geez, Fang, like to scare the crap out of me!". The cat meowed loudly, rubbing up against Carl's leg. "Yeah, I know, supper's late."

Carl got inside the cabin, continuously tripping over the hungry cat. Grabbing the bag of cat food from the cupboard, he took a handful and dumped it into a small tin. Most of it missed the tin and spilled across the wooden plank floor. Fang savagely cleaned the floor up in no time.

Carl turned his attention to himself now that Fang was fed. He wanted a drink of water and to brush his teeth. He remembered that his water container was empty. He had been in too much of a hurry that morning to refill it. Reluctantly he grabbed the five-gallon bucket, walked out to the five-foot-tall hand pump, and set the bucket on the log under the spigot. After a couple of pumps, cool clear water gushed into the bucket. He took the toothbrush from his back pocket, dipped it into the cool water, and brushed his teeth as he filled the bucket. The moon was almost full, rising over the tree line, lighting the path back to the cabin. He dipped the toothbrush one more time in the bucket, swirled the residual toothpaste around in his mouth once more, and spit before going back into the cabin. He lifted the heavy bucket to the makeshift kitchen counter. Some water splashed over as he set it heavily on the counter. Carl brushed the spilled water off the counter and wiped his hand on his dirty pants.

Moonlight barely lit up the inside of the cabin. He sat on the edge of the bed, looking at the five-gallon bucket sitting on the kitchen counter. He had worked hard this year to get that hand pump. That had been a big goal for him. They had drilled the well and installed the freestanding hand pump only a month earlier. *Man, I am glad I don't have to pack water from the creek anymore,* he thought.

He got one boot off and the other untied before he fell over asleep in his bed. Fang curled up next to his head.

As I watched Carl weaving his Harley down the back road towards his cabin, I reminisced how I met him. He and I were on the Department of Lands fire crew. Carl was known locally as a recluse since he lived on a remote section of land in a one-room cabin. He pretty much kept to himself, and most folks in the little resort town preferred that. He didn't have running water in his house, so his clothes were not always clean by their standards. He always smelled of woodsmoke, because that was how he cooked his meals. No one knew much about him. He just showed up one day and kept to himself.

One lady described Carl as a lab experiment that had gone awry. He and I joked about that often. I am not sure why, but we hit it off the first day we met. He was probably the toughest guy I have ever met. One time I got a little cocky with him, and we started slap boxing. He cleaned my clock in seconds, ending it with a well-placed kick that just about broke my leg.

Carl was tough, but he had to be from the beginning. When he was seventeen, he volunteered to fight in Vietnam. He was a member of the 101st Airborne Division. He saw a lot of combat. One thing he often joked about was "I have never been scared, but I have run backward passed people who were."

He served three terms in Vietnam. He probably would have served four terms if they would have let him. On his last tour, a grenade went off near him, injuring him badly. The surgeon put a metal plate in his head, and he lost most of his hearing. After that, Carl learned to read lips. If you wanted him to hear what you said, you needed to be in front of him or chances are he wouldn't hear you. Sometimes I think he used that to his advantage.

It was as if Carl had a death wish or something. That is why he kept going back to Vietnam for another tour time after time. That, and he was just good at what they sent him there for. After the war, Vietnam vets were not welcomed back home like they should have been. It was an unpopular war, and they were not treated very well at all. Both the war itself and how they were treated when they returned had a detrimental impact on many of them. It got into their head. Many became like Carl, a recluse. North Idaho was a magnet for many vets. They could hide in the backwoods, live off the grid, and survive okay. There were pockets of vets scattered across North Idaho. They formed strong alliances among themselves.

Carl and I often used to drink and play pool after work. He used to open up after he started drinking and shared a little of his past with me. I think he needed to get it out. Hanging out and getting to know his character, I pieced a lot together.

When Carl returned from Vietnam, I think the rejection hit him hard, so he rebelled hard. He started riding with the Hells Angels in California. It was a rough way of life, but they accepted and respected him, and that was what he was searching for. Everyone wants that. However, while he never came right out and said it, I don't think that lifestyle suited him. He liked the fact that the vest he wore scared folks, but I think that was a reaction to the rejection he was feeling. He pushed people away so they wouldn't hurt him.

He told me one night that he and some of his "brothers" went into a bar, somewhere in Ohio. A local biker gang was also in the bar, and one of the locals hit on one of their girls. Things got ugly and unfortunate. Carl didn't admit to anything; he just said that he had to make himself scarce after that night. He ditched his vest along the road and landed somewhere in Montana, where he got a job on a remote ranch as a ranch hand.

Carl was strong and had a good work ethic. He holed up there for a while until he saved enough money to buy the land in North Idaho. I saw how hard Carl worked and how, when he set his mind to get something, nothing would deter him. Like how hard he worked to get water at the cabin. I felt bad to see him skipping lunch so he could have water, so I "accidentally" made an extra sandwich for when he "forgot" to make lunch. Lunch was important to Carl. Me too, I suppose. Lunches reminded me of an incident Carl and I had gone through earlier that summer.

Our crew got called to a fire south of Sandpoint, up Blacktail Creek. It was a windy night in the middle of August. We had been thinning trees all day when we got the call. By the time we got to the fire, the sun was going down. Since we were an initial attack crew, they sent us to the more active section of the fire to try to get a line in front of it.

Our crew was efficient. We all were adept at sawing, but because Carl couldn't hear all that well, we usually kept him at the back of the crew. With him behind swinging a pulaski really kept the crew moving! We were working up an especially fast-moving section of the fire when a guy came up the fire line from behind us with lunches. We stopped to visit with the guy, and he mentioned how the fire behavior had been so unpredictable that night. He said for some reason, it was difficult for the overhead team to contact us over the radio. They assumed we were on the wrong channel or in a dead spot. After we synchronized channels with the guy, he headed back down the fire line to base camp.

About that time a call came over the radio that the fire was blowing up. It said that if anyone knew where the Priest Lake crew was, to get them out of there. When we tried to respond, no one answered back. In a panic, we took off running down the fire line. It was nighttime, and we didn't know the lay of the land, so we were essentially bluffing it. Suddenly Carl stopped and yelled, "Hey, we left our lunches back there!" Kevin, our crew boss, asked if there was anyone who wanted to go back and get them. Both Carl and I volunteered.

We turned and ran as fast as we could back to the spot where the lunches had been dropped off and stuffed them in our fire packs.

Suddenly we were surrounded by flames leaping fifteen to twenty feet in the air all around us. The whole forest lit up as if it were the middle of the day. An unnerving roar, louder than anything I had ever heard, sounded below us. Surely it was the noise, but it seemed as though the ground was shaking. Walls of fire raced towards us. A surge of adrenaline kicked in as we ran back towards the crew. The night transformed into a brilliant orange glow everywhere we looked. Shadows no longer existed. And the roar! The noise was deafening. Trees were popping all around us. The fire was making a run and getting into the tops of the trees. Flames were beginning to lick trees over our head, bursting into flames. The heat was intense, it felt like our flesh was starting to melt. Fortunately, we had gloves, hardhats and fire shirts to somewhat protect our bodies, but our faces were exposed. Carl and I raised our tools to shield our skin from the intense heat. I distinctly remember thinking as we were running to save our lives. "Boy, this was a stupid!"

When we caught up with the others, our shirts and gloves were steaming.

Boy, was that a night! We ran from fire the whole night. I shook my head and fell back into my bunk, immediately falling asleep.

The next morning the sunrise woke me up early. I knew the marina wouldn't be open yet, but I knew that Tim would be up, and he would have coffee on. I walked down to the edge of the lake and out to the end of the dock. It was a beautiful September morning. You could feel the crispness of fall, and the faint smell of woodsmoke intermingled with the scent of the mountains and the lake was in the air. Smoke from nearby cabins drifted low on the water, and leaves were beginning to change from green into bright yellows, oranges and reds.

Behind me, I heard the bells on the door clang as Tim unlocked the door. Even though the marina wasn't open yet, it was his way of inviting me in for coffee.

I swung my leg over the bar stool as Tim slid a hot cup of black coffee in front of me. "I wonder if Carl made it home okay." he said.

"I hope so. He was weaving pretty good down the back road. Sure hope he didn't hit a tree."

"Or a moose," Tim replied, sliding the front section of the *Spokesman-Review* towards me.

We both read the newspaper for a while in silence. After Tim had finished the Sports section, he asked: "What are you up to today?"

"Well, I was hoping Nick would be down here so we could go fishing. He just got back yesterday from that project fire over in Montana." I answered. "I'll give him another hour of sleep and then get his sorry butt up and going."

Just then there was a commotion at the front door. Carl pulled up in his brown Jeep and burst through both doors with the bells clamoring. He was covered from head to toe in blood and soot.

Tim and I turned in shock. Both of us said in unison. "What happened to you?"

Carl plopped down on the bar stool next to me. His hair was messed up, with blood in it. He even had blood on his glasses.

"Man, I got home last night, and the bear had made a mess with my refrigerator again. I got in the house and fell into bed. I was tired. My glasses fell off me and were under the bed. I had a dickens of a time finding them.

"When I woke up, I heard this terrible hissing and yowling sound. At first, I couldn't figure out what it was. It was barely light out, but something heavy was sitting on my feet. All I could see was a brown blur. Then I felt Fang next to my head all puffed up, growling like crazy. I realized then the bear had broken the window and was sitting on my feet, so I grabbed the .44 magnum on the nightstand next to me and unloaded into the bear. The percussion was so strong, it knocked the bear off the bed into the woodstove, and out from under the stove pipe. The stove pipe collapsed in the house, and there is black soot everywhere. I guess I am gonna have to clean my house!"

Carl shook his head in disbelief. Tim pushed a hot cup of coffee towards Carl.

"Thanks, Tim," Carl said, taking a short sip. "Boy, I am sure glad I didn't have a fire in the stove last night! I have been lighting it every night this last week to keep the nip off."

"Where is the bear now?" I asked.

Carl laughed "I had to drag him outside to gut him out! Fang was still puffed up when I left. Poor cat!"

Carl lived a remote, reclusive life by choice. Much of that was due to what he experienced when he came back from Vietnam. He struggled inside to find a normalcy with his past. Like Carl, many vets come back from wars haunted by things they have seen. No matter what they do, they can't seem to shake they have experienced. It's stuck in their subconscious.

My dad used to duck every time he heard a loud noise. As kids, we always thought it was funny. It was an instinctive response to being shot at. Dad never talked much about the Korean War, but after he died, my uncle explained what Dad's assignment had been. He was assigned to go ahead of the front line with a radio to triangulate the enemy's position. He constantly had bullets flying around him, and that experience tormented him the rest of his life.

I have a friend who was married to a Vietnam Vet for thirty-eight years. Carol told me, Mike had terrifying dreams almost every night. She said it seemed like he was always running from something. Like something was after him. She asked him one morning what he was running from, and he had no recollection.

Carl often joked about running backward past people who were scared. He joked about it, but I know he had some deep underlying issues. He had seen things no eighteen year old should ever see and then the rejection he experienced when he came back home from Vietnam was unbearable. Imagine going off to war when you are still barely a kid. You believe in your heart that you are serving your country as any person would. Then you come home to rejection from the country you were fighting to serve.

The combination of all of that becomes a prison in your mind you can't escape from. Your subconscious mind tries to find some common ground to stand on, but it becomes a vicious circle.

Carl had everyone buffaloed in the little town where he lived. He had a gruff appearance that made most folks keep away. He was rough and could be crude at times, but when you peeled away the layers, he was a tender, bighearted man. Carl was one of the nicest guys I have ever met. The fear of rejection caused him to lash out so people wouldn't hurt him anymore. Carl had surrounded himself with a huge wall of protection.

There are a lot of people with similar hurts inflicted from society not just Veterans. They have been rejected, beaten down, and tramped on physically as well as mentally. Those pains create walls of protection from fear, entrapping them in an internal prison. Some walls can get so thick, the only thing that can penetrate is Jesus.

The Bible says, "Perfect love casts out fear." So, what is perfect love? People aren't perfect by a long shot. They are the ones who caused the hurt. Jesus is the only one who is perfect. So, Jesus casts out fear.

It stands to reason that if Jesus is in your heart, then "perfect love" would be there too. When Jesus resides inside of you, He works to break down the walls from the inside out, peeling back the built-up layers little by little with His perfect love. He knows better than you do how you got where you are, and He knows what it takes to heal you. What is cool is, you don't need to do anything but trust Him. Initially that is a big step, but after you do it, He will do everything else. If you allow Jesus to come into your heart, He will, in His time, break down that inner wall and His "perfect love" will shine through the crack He opened. Gradually, it will open and let all the pain and fear leak out of you.

Carol, shared with me the struggles she endured being married to a veteran suffering from PTSD. She said that in the last few years of their marriage before Mike died, Mike finally came to grips with it. After the kids had all left home, Mike diligently sought the Lord regarding the internal struggle he had struggled with for so many years. She says that she watched the change in her husband and that those were, without a doubt, the best years of their marriage. She finally got the man she loved.

We all react differently to fear. Some folks run from it, some laugh and others fight. I guess there is a time where each reaction is fitting. If fear has set up camp in your heart, it's time to tear down those prison walls and let the Son shine in!

Hitching a Ride

Mathew 10:28

And do not fear those who kill the body but cannot kill the soul. But rather fear Him who is able to destroy both body and soul in hell.

"I have a craving for seafood," my new friend Richard announced.

I looked at his bright blue eyes. The round wire-rim glasses enhanced them in the late winter's bright sunshine. His glasses couldn't help but emphasize his disproportionally large nose, passed down from his Jewish forefathers. The bushy red hair and beard fulfilled the picture-perfect description of a young Jewish man, or at least everything I knew about anyone Jewish. That picture had been painted so clearly with the aid of television in the mid-seventies. It still left a lot of questions for me. I often wondered why everyone hated the Jews so bad. When the subject came up, and people made fun of the Jewish people, I had to remain quiet and listen because I was completely ignorant. I gleaned what I could, and unfortunately, this biased source is where I got most of my misinformation on the subject. Still, it didn't make any sense to me. Shoot, Israel was some little podunk country smaller than the state of New Jersey. Why did they ruffle everyone's feathers? Why did the Germans want to kill them off and annihilate the whole population? Seriously, were they that big of a threat? So, they dressed like a bunch of geeks and had weird eccentricities about the food they ate. Big deal! It always seemed like they got a raw deal on everything, and I wanted to find out why. That was part of the reason I befriended Richard, and he had a dry sense of humor. You had to be on your toes to catch it sometimes.

"I have a buddy in Wenatchee. He just got back from the coast with a cooler full of salmon and halibut," Richard continued. "He invited me over for a couple of days."

My taste buds were salivating. It didn't help that it was just about lunchtime. "You lucky dog! I would jump on that opportunity if I were you," I responded in envy.

"Well, I am hitchhiking over there as soon as we get laid off. C'mon with me. My buddy won't mind at all."

I thought it over in my mind. I didn't have anything going on for a week or so. I had planned to visit my buddy Nick in Coeur d'Alene for a while before work started back up at Bozeman Brick, Block and Tile. I could swing by and see him on the way back. By the end of the day, I'd agreed to go along. We decided to leave after work on Wednesday and spend the night wherever we ended up on the side of the road. Both of us were on a tight budget and would be traveling light.

We agreed that there would be no motels. We would be roughing it.

I parked my rig at my girlfriend Karen's place. She would give both of us a ride to the interstate. When Richard showed up at the house, the look on Karen's face showed that she deeply wondered about my critical thinking. Her eyes spoke volumes. When she covered her eyes and shook her head, I tried to take a step back to see what she was seeing on her side.

Richard was dressed, like, well, Richard. He had tan slacks on with black loafers, a black belt, a red-and-black wool plaid button-down shirt, and a heavy green coat. His bushy red hair and beard didn't add much to his skinny frame. Honestly, he looked like a Jewish geek with highwater pants and white socks dropped into a logger's shirt. A skinny gnome with thick, wire-rimmed glasses, going to a Bar Mitzvah in a remote town in northwest Montana. Yeah, I could see her point, this journey could be a long one; he had a blue backpack with a super-clean blue sleeping bag tied to the bottom that had never seen the ground.

I wore Levi's with cowboy boots, a blue-and-white flannel shirt, and an insulated Levi's jacket. I had a large brass belt buckle on a brown belt. My favorite red backpack had a blue sleeping bag tucked into a bag that was tied to the frame. Then, of course, I had my lucky fishing pole and a sign that said *Wenatchee* and *Please*. I had a rule about hitchhiking. Always dress nice, shave, have a sign that gives the destination and says "Please" and always, always have a fishing pole in your hand. My theory was that everyone loved fishing. It piqued their curiosity of where you were going fishing, and they knew you couldn't be a threat if you had a fishing pole.

I looked at Richard and then at myself and back to Karen, who was peering from under her hands, trying not to laugh. I guess we did look like we were from two different parts of the planet, but it was too late to cancel the trip.

Have you ever been getting ready to leave on a trip and you had a little bit of a stomachache telling you not to go, but you ignored it? That is what was going on.

It took us forever to get a ride out of Bozeman, which was a little embarrassing. I mean, we couldn't even get out of town! People I knew drove by. Waving. Both directions. That was very unusual for me. Whenever I hitchhiked, I always got a ride in a matter of minutes.

We finally got a ride in the back of a pickup to Lookout Pass. It was dark when we got there, so we decided to spend the night. It happened to be the perfect spot in the dark. There was a place off the road with a nice level place to sleep. There was an open gravel area to build a fire to heat a can of beans. As hungry as I was, the beans went along perfectly with a mashed peanut butter and jelly sandwich. *Making a complete loaf of Wonder Bread into those sandwiches was such a great idea*, I mused.

The next morning, I woke to the sound of traffic on the highway. As I peered out of my sleeping bag, I noticed a small spider diligently building an intricate web right in front of me. He must have been working most of the night on his project, and it was just about complete. The sunlight broke the skyline and brilliantly lit up his work of art. The little spider seemed to stop and admire his hard work. I slowly slipped my hand into my sleeping bag to pull my Nikon camera out to capture this prestigious event. Using a shallow depth of field, I focused in on the spider and how the lines spread out in all directions, blurring into the brilliant sunlight. Suddenly an incomprehensively loud air horn sounded from behind me, breaking all focus on the spider. Jumping to my feet. I turned to see a large state dump truck approaching quickly towards our campsite. Really? Of all the nerve, I thought, standing there in my boxers. My anger turned to anguish when I realized we had camped at the entrance to the state gravel stockpile and they just happened to be stockpiling. I looked over at Richard and saw him pulling his tan slacks over his skinny white legs. His bushy red hair was flat on one side of his head. I tried my best not to laugh as he frantically searched for his wire-rimmed glasses, squinting hard to comprehend the approaching danger. Before long, I couldn't contain myself and burst into laughter at the situation and how fast he was getting dressed. He didn't find the humor in the situation. I quickly learned he wasn't a morning person.

It was rather embarrassing each time a dump truck of gravel came through while we packed our gear up. Maybe three trucks went by, but it seemed like two hours of embarrassment. That embarrassment pushed us on down the road a bit to avoid the hysterical laughter and honking each time they passed. To add to the humiliation, it took forever to get a ride. I began to suspect that maybe it was Richard who was causing the problem of not getting a ride. I suspected that he was thinking the same thing about me. We stopped talking to each other. The trip began to become tedious.

Suddenly a pickup came by, instantly removing the negative thoughts.

The driver motioned to the back of the truck and hollered out the window that he was going to Post Falls. Richard and I hopped in the back of the truck and leaned against the cab to lessen the wind resistance. The trip had begun in humiliation but was back on track. Within a little more than an hour, we were back in the same situation, sitting on the side of the road. We waited for several long hours, not speaking. Finally, Richard suggested that we split up to see if we could get a ride faster. He was thinking the same thing I was. I agreed, and just as he started to walk down the freeway, another truck stopped. This time a lady with a couple of kids pulled over. I went to the window, and she said that she was headed to Moses Lake, but there was no room in the front. We would have to ride in the back.

We asked her if she could drop us off somewhere in Moses Lake where we could get something to eat. She obliged and dropped us off at a burger joint at the edge of town. I noticed that everywhere we went people stared at us. We were an unusual pair I surmised. When we had finished eating, we started to hike down the road towards the freeway entrance. When we heard a car approaching from behind us, we stuck out our thumbs.

I think we were both surprised when a van pulled over. After the hardship we had getting this far, we were less selective on our ride. Richard hopped in the van, and I followed, not hesitating. The strong smell of marijuana hit my nostrils as I and shut the door. A very large, burly man with long hair and a beard turned and asked me,

"Where you headed?"

I watched his eyes glance at the Nikon camera on my neck. I pulled my backpack tighter to my chest. I couldn't hold his cold, intense stare and looked out at the countryside passing by. "Wenatchee." Richard answered.

"What a coincidence! That's where we are going!" All three of the large men started laughing. I wanted to throw up.

A longhaired man with a motorcycle-gang vest turned around from the passenger seat with a joint in his hand. "Wanna hit?" he asked.

I looked at the tightly rolled joint with the billowing smoke rolling off the end of it. "No, thanks."

The driver turned and looked me in the eye and with a menacing growl said, "Take a hit."

Richard grabbed the joint, took a long pull and handed it to the big guy to his left. He took a long pull on it and held it to the point of coughing. He coughed so hard, he drooled spittle out of his mouth, and he wiped it off quickly. The driver watched me menacingly from the rearview mirror. I had made an enemy, and I knew it. This was going to be a long trip.

A sour feeling rose up from deep in my stomach, working through my body down to my bones. I began to wish I had never gone on this trip. I would have given anything to be back in Montana.

The man sitting next to Richard passed the joint to the driver, hitting him on his shoulder. The driver took the joint from him and took a long pull. Smoke from the end swirled up into his eyes, and he squinted, continuing to stare at me through the rearview mirror. When he was finished, he passed the joint back to me. "Here, take a hit!" he demanded.

I looked at the little joint in his large hand. He wore a large copper bracelet on his wrist, and there was a blue-green tattoo hidden beneath the hair on his arm. The illustration of a snake encircling a skull and crossbones seemed appropriate at the time. He was Satan himself and offering me the mark of the beast.

"I don't smoke," I said sternly, looking him squarely in the eye. Anger was rising in me now.

The silence in the van became thick and laced with mortal danger. When he saw I wouldn't take the joint, he shoved it at the man in the passenger seat. The man flinched, cowering towards the door. The driver didn't wait for the passenger to take the joint, and it fell precariously into the passenger's lap. He jumped to the side, frantically retrieving the joint and putting out the cherry before it burned him.

Furious rage built up inside of the huge man driving. His face was turning red. I didn't know if it was the pot or his temper. I assumed it was a lethal mixture of both. Fortunately, I was just out of his reach. I sensed that he wanted nothing more than to feel my throat collapsing in his giant hand. I could feel Richard shaking next to me. He was much closer than I to the danger.

We drove in silence for what seemed like an eternity. I watched as the barren countryside went by. The silence broke when the driver asked what kind of camera I had.

"It's a Nikon," I said.

"Let me see it," he demanded.

I wanted to throw up. I knew if I gave it to him, I wouldn't get it back. I tucked it close to my stomach and nervously wrapped my backpack straps tightly in my left hand.

"I don't think so," I said, glancing over at Richard. Richard's blue eyes were filled with fear. His line of sight shifted from my eyes to the door handle. I saw with my peripheral vision; Richard shift his hands to his backpack.

The driver grabbed a giant bowie knife laying on the center console between him and the passenger and picking it up, drove it deep into the foam on the console. "Give me the camera!" he screamed.

I noticed that we were pulling away from a four-way stop and picking up speed quickly. I reached over and pulled hard on the handle, releasing the door. It slid easily on the rollers. I pulled my backpack up in my face and dove out the door, preparing to roll into the borrow pit. Richard was right behind me. Both of us recovered from the roll and were on our feet, running. The van slowed down at first until the man sitting next to

Richard had pulled the door shut. All three laughed as they sped off.

Richard and I kept running across the bright green wheat field. When we finally stopped, we both bent over, trying to catch our breath. My legs were shaking uncontrollably. I looked at Richard bent over with his hands on his knees. His bushy red hair rustled in the breeze. His eyes were filled with fear.

I rose up, standing upright gasping for air. "I am done," I said, between gasps. "I am going back to Montana."

"Okay, I am going to Wenatchee," he replied.

There was an uncanny silence between us. I couldn't even call him a friend. I didn't ever get to know him. It was weird. It just was. I felt like I should have some feeling, but there was nothing. About a quarter of a mile away, I noticed a freight train slowing down on the tracks. It was pointed in the direction of Montana.

I muttered under my breath, "My ride's here!"

I picked up my backpack and started running towards the train.

As I neared, I saw a man walking along the tracks. He looked like he was checking the connections or something on the train. He stopped when he saw me coming. The man was an older gentleman. His face was kind, but anyone's face would have been kind in comparison to the demon-possessed guy I had just encountered.

I was still shaking from the previous encounter. I spewed out what had happened and pleaded with the man to please let me ride away from where we were. He listened to my story with empathy. When I finished, he explained that it was company policy not to allow anyone to ride on the train other than company employees. He said they enforced it strictly.

My shoulders dropped in despair. I looked around at the expansive grain fields around me. "I gotta get out of here." I said more to myself than to him.

"I don't always see, if say, someone hops a ride after I get in the engine compartment," and he winked at me.

"Oh, thank you!" I said.

"For what?" He smiled.

"Where is this train going? I asked.

"Great Falls," he said, looking back towards the train. "You want to make sure that the doors don't close as you are going. They are very heavy, and some are very hard to get back open. When we park them, some cars might not get used for up to a month or so. If the door happened to close, and no one knew you were in there, you could freeze or even starve to death."

I nodded, absorbing every word he said. I was so thankful for a ride away from this place in a different mode other than hitchhiking.

"Where are you headed? he asked.

"Anywhere but here!" I said, "Bozeman is home, but I might swing by and see a buddy in Coeur d'Alene. I need to get somewhere to calm down for a while."

"We won't be going near Bozeman or stopping in Coeur d'Alene, but we will stop briefly in Spokane to drop off a few cars." He looked me over and said. "You better tuck that camera away when we get driving through Spokane. There's a good population of homeless there. You are going to stick out like a sore thumb. If I were you, I would keep myself scarce as we pull into the train yard. They will spot you, and if you give them a half a chance, they won't think twice of knocking you in the head. As soon as we stop, get off the train and head south. So, get off the train on the right side of the car and high tail it out of the yard. Maybe you can get your buddy to come over from Coeur d'Alene to pick you up."

"Okay," I nodded, taking in all the information. This trip seemed to have snares on every corner. I thought about what he said but could not remember what Nick's new phone number was. I had a vague idea of the apartment complex where he lived.

I thanked him, and he proceeded to check the remainder of the cars for problems. He had gone about fifteen steps when he turned and warned me again. "If someone else sees you, they will kick you off the train, so keep out of sight."

"Okay," I said. "Thank you!"

"Seriously, watch out for bums. They will kill you." His words made the hair stand up on the back of my neck. I'd had my fill of excitement on this trip.

After he moved on, I threw my backpack into an empty car. Then I followed by jumping in on my belly and rolling in the rest of the way. The floor was rough hardwood. I stood back in the corner away from the door. It was cold in the shade. It would be even colder when we got to moving fifty miles per hour. I was anxious to get going, hoping no one would catch me and kick me off the train. I needed this ride back home. I opened my backpack, removed my wool stocking cap, and tucked my Nikon safely in its place. Suddenly a loud noise shuddered down through all the cars and the train began to move. As it gained momentum, I wanted to look outside, but the fear of being caught prevented me.

I sat back and took a big sigh of relief when suddenly a dingy, army-issue-green pack flew in the door, landing in the center of the car. I stood staring at it in shock when an unkempt man jumped in the door of the car on his stomach and frantically wiggled his way into the car.

I flattened back against the railroad car. A thousand thoughts ran through my mind, particularly the ones about watching out for bums and how they would probably kill me. One thought that seemed like the right thing to do was going over to help him get in, but the other competing thought was quickly kicking him in the chest and pushing him off the train. The two conflicting thoughts caused me to stand there, motionless, holding my breath.

He wiggled himself in and rolled over on his butt with his legs dangling out the car door. He still hadn't seen me. I didn't know what to do or say. He sat there for the longest time. The train picked up speed and began to rock back and forth. The short, stocky man skootched back on his butt before rolling onto his side to stand up. Then he saw me. He was as surprised as I was when I had first seen him. His alarm and wariness made me think he had gotten the same memo about the hazards of hopping a freight train. I nodded at him, and he slowly nodded back, eying me carefully, and then he glanced out at the ground, passing by quickly. I was trying to figure out what was going on in his head. Was he thinking of jumping off the train, or was he thinking of trying to throw me off? That last thought unnerved me. I'd had enough people pushing me around for one day. I grabbed my fishing pole firmly in my hand. He was going to have a fight on his hand if he chose that route.

He must have read my body language well because he chose to sit on the front portion of the car some distance from me. I sat down near the car door, so I could watch the countryside pass by. I had never ridden a train and wanted to savor this experience.

The rocking of the train had a calming effect on me, but when the man stood up to move closer to the door, my body tensed up. He had his eye on me too. Neither of us trusted the other. The man had some gray hair starting to show. His red-and-white plaid coat was heavy and quite soiled. It looked warm but had seen a few cold days. I wondered why he was on the journey he was on. Where was he going? He wanted to sit in the warm spring sun and enjoy the ride like I did. When I opened my backpack, he kept one eye fixed on me. I dug down deep in the main compartment and found a couple of flattened peanut butter and blackberry jam sandwiches. I inspected one of them carefully. The blackberry had soaked through, and it looked like a black-and-blue glob of dough. I lifted the one that most resembled a sandwich and asked, "Peanut butter and jelly sandwich? They are a little smashed, but they're good!"

He smiled and nodded. "*Si, señor! Gracias.*"

I tossed the sandwich over to him and watched him as he ate it. He was hungry. I enjoyed how he graciously savored every morsel. I had made an ally.

He started to say something in Spanish, but I stopped him with my hand. "Sorry, me *no comprende.*"

He nodded and smiled, lifting the remainder of the sandwich.

The ride was beautiful, rocking back and forth over the rails. Such a different perspective than from the highway. The repetitious *klunklunk, klunklunk, klunklunk* as the car went over the rails was soothing, but the wind was cold. I pulled my coat in closer and pulled my legs tighter to my body.

Gradually the countryside morphed into suburbia. More cars were on the highway and I saw the drivers noticed me. I backed out of sight. At the inner-city view, anxiety rose in me. Noticeably the train slowed down. I kept back out of view, and yet I wanted to visualize the escape route. As we entered the train yard, homeless people appeared everywhere. It was like a city. They were all people just like me, but the game had changed. I sensed their hopelessness seeping into my bones and a chill went down deep into my heart. There was a numbness in their intense stares. Hunger and desperation were very apparent. I felt like a gazelle alone on the plains of the Serengeti, surrounded by predators. I had to run the gauntlet without being taken down. A vision of how a wolf pack drags down its prey passed through my mind. The palms of my hands were sweating, and my mouth was dry. A group of five men standing over a barrel fire turned and watched me.

One of them nodded towards me in conversation. Seconds later, a couple of them left the circle, heading swiftly in the direction I was going. My heart pounded loudly. I was out of my element. I no longer worried about the man I had been riding with in the train. A civilized danger surrounded me. I felt like everyone was moving in my direction. I needed to get going. I picked a path across a dozen or so train tracks to an opening through some very rough-looking buildings. The train was just about to stop as I put my backpack on. With my fishing pole firmly grasped in my right hand, I jumped from the train. Running across the tracks was awkward with the heavy backpack on my back. It was top-heavy, making running difficult. The last thing I wanted to do was to fall. I could imagine them ganging up on me, surrounding me on every side, taking a shot at me until I couldn't defend myself anymore.

Eventually I broke through the dark confines of the train yard and burst into the inner city. It was five o'clock and bumper-to-bumper traffic. Cars were going in every direction. I had no idea where I was, or which way Coeur d'Alene was. The noise was deafening after the quiet, peaceful ride on the train. Cars raced by me. I stuck my thumb out and hustled to get out of this crazy, busy city. The traffic stopped for a stoplight, and a car next to me honked, making me jump. I looked in the car's direction, and the driver waved me over. He rolled down the window and asked where I was going. I told him Coeur d'Alene, and he opened the door.

"Whereabouts in Coeur d'Alene are you going?" he asked.

"I don't know the address." I hesitated, looking the man over carefully.

He caught my cautiousness and smiled warmly, moving a briefcase to the back seat. Then he looked at the light, which had turned green, and back at me.

The car behind us honked impatiently as I put my backpack in the back seat. I gave him a shot of stink eye before getting in the front seat. Turning to the driver, I said, "I hope you're not a crazy person, because I can't handle much more excitement today."

He laughed "Well, that is debatable. Some folks think I am crazy, and I wonder that myself some days. I am a pastor downtown at the Mission. You don't look like the typical guy on the street. I can give you a ride to wherever you need to go."

I wanted to hug him. Finally, I could relax. It felt like a huge load had been removed from my shoulders.

When Richard and I "took the dive" there was no thinking about it. It was the only option. Everything fell into place perfectly. Each of us is given an opportunity to escape from a similar situation in this life, but it requires us to act.

There would be no reasoning with that deranged drug-induced animal. His only intent was to inflict harm.

Unlike an animal that might be protecting its babies or in a fight for food or its life, this character's primary goal in existence was to inflict fear and harm. It is selfish in that producing fear gives him power. This is precisely what Satan does in our lives. His goal is to rob, steal, and destroy. By doing so, he can paralyze you with fear, which causes destruction and blocks you to come to know God. Satan knows that, and that is why he does it. You see, there is a very real battle going on daily in each of our lives, whether we realize it or not. It is a battle for our souls.

Which, in turn, leads to the reason Satan has been trying to annihilate the Jewish people. The Jews are God's chosen people. That infuriates Satan. That is the only reason. We and they have something that Satan has lost. It is the option to have a relationship with God.

When God sent His son Jesus to earth, it was to provide a way to protect us from Satan, the liar, the deceiver, the destroyer of our souls. The Jews figured Jesus came to earth to exalt them as a people, to make them a great nation. God did that, but just not in the way that the Jews expected. You ever notice how when you expect how something is going to turn out a certain way, it never does? It's the same thing.

When the Jews rejected Jesus by crucifying Him on the cross, God used the death of His son Jesus to open the gates of Heaven for the rest of us regular folk to get into heaven. That's great, but here is a catch. First, the only way you can do it is through faith. You must believe that Jesus died for your sins. That is where the Jews messed up. They didn't believe, and that is why they are going through all of this on earth. Oh, there is one more thing.

There is an expiration date on this offer, and it is not completely clear when it will expire. There is a reason for that too. God knew that we people, in general, have a propensity to procrastinate. Consequently, the call to action is immediate. The other option is to ride in the van with that deranged tormentor until he gets his hand around your throat.

Once you get in with the right driver, a huge load is lifted from your shoulders. All you need to do is ride along and let Him do the driving.

My Prayer, right here, right now, is that God touch you deeply with this book propelling you into the deepest, most loving relationship you have ever experienced.

God Bless You!

Acknowledgments

First, all glory goes to God, the Father. Without His prompting, this book would not have been written. He never ceases to amaze me.

Jenny Leo – Jenny is so gifted with her editing wisdom and has blessed this book with her talent.

Catherine Thom – Catherine and her family have been such a great role model in Christ. I appreciate her sense of humor, wisdom and tenacity for the Lord.

Jenny Jones – Jenny is the epitome of encouragement. I so appreciate her love for the Lord and her love for every person she meets to have a loving relationship with Jesus. She is a true evangelist and what a good friend she is!

Laurie Koga – Laurie has been my side-kick a majority of my life. She has done her best to keep me out of trouble and that has been a full-time job. I appreciate her honesty, accountability and value her sense of humor and friendship.

Sarah Jones – Sarah is like a daughter to me. I am so thankful for her suggestions, sense of humor, encouragement and friendship.

Nick Nicolls – I can't seem to write a story without having Nick's name in it somewhere. I have so many stories I could tell, but, so does he. I appreciate his ear and patience while I relentlessly work out the stories in these books.

If this book has helped make a positive change in your life, I would love to hear your story. You can contact me through the website. www.rustyironranchllc.com

Thanks and God Bless YOU!
Bill

If you enjoyed this book, check out these other books written by William H. Cox at:
www.rustyironranchllc.com

The Last Cast
Proactively fishing with grace

ISBN-13: 978-0692095577 (Rusty Iron Ranch, LLC)
ISBN-10: 0692095578

The unconditional love of
A Dog's Love

ISBN-13: 978-0692716366 (Rusty Iron Ranch, LLC)
ISBN-10: 069271636X

Skies Are Not Cloudy All Day
Is God trying to get your attention?

ISBN-13: 978-1-312-93832-8 (Rusty Iron Ranch, LLC)

Made in the USA
Lexington, KY
25 November 2019